THE PUBLIC VOIDS OF THE POST-SOVIET CITY

OWEN
HATHERLEY

CONTENTS

- 7 AN EMPTY SPACE CREATES A RICHLY FILLED TIME—INTRODUCTION
- 26 THE STEPPE STARTS HERE
ALEXANDERPLATZ, BERLIN
- 38 CONSTRUCTIVIST SQUARE
PLOSHCHAD SVOBODY, KHARKOV
- 50 FORMER SQUARE
PLAC DEFILAD, WARSAW
- 58 SQUARE AS SMALL-TOWN SIMULACRUM
STARY RYNEK, ŁÓDŹ
- 66 SQUARE OF THE INDUSTRIAL METROPOLIS
RYNEK, KATOWICE
- 77 THE NON-ALIGNED SQUARE
TRG REPUBLIKE, LJUBLJANA
- 85 CHEKIST SQUARE
PLOSHCHAD LYBIDSKA, KIEV
- 93 SQUARE BETWEEN COSMOS & CHAOS
PLOSHCHAD GAGARINA, MOSCOW
- 101 THE SQUARE ABOLISHES ITSELF
POTSDAMER PLATZ, BERLIN
- 111 THE SQUARE AFTER THE SQUARE
—EPILOGUE

AN EMPTY SPACE CREATES A RICHLY FILLED TIME

INTRODUCTION

ACROSS THE PLAZA

A wide open space, a big city-centre square. When you stand in the middle of it the wind lashes ruthlessly at your face. Surrounding you are buildings, huge things of granite and concrete on a strict axial plan, governmental offices no doubt. You are probably being watched—your presence registered by a bored CCTV operative nursing a coffee in a nearby office—but you know that just over twenty years ago you might have been watched instead by a secret police force. Which can give you a frisson, if that kind of thing is to your taste. The square itself has some movement in it—people are smoking under some awnings in their lunch break, someone else is begging, the kiosks of 'informal' commerce have a bustle around them. If you're in the former East Germany or the former Soviet Union, there's also something more inanimate—an exhortative statue of Marx or Lenin may be keeping you company, or gesturing aggressively at you for your sloth. Elsewhere, the punctuation is provided by more traditional monuments—a warlord, a Corinthian column, a bewhiskered general. But the feeling of immense, unused space still endures, and that's the source of that wind, the biting wind that sooner or later will force you back indoors. Oh the square is interesting, for sure, a three-dimensional survivor from a dead age, a museum piece. But it's a mistake, nonetheless. You certainly couldn't learn anything from it.

AN EMPTY SPACE CREATES A RICHLY...

There are few things in urbanism today so unfashionable as that wide open sense of space. Looking round the subjects of this text—at the likes of Berlin-Alexanderplatz, Warsaw's Plac Defilad, Katowice's Rynek—the first response of most contemporary urban planners would be a feeling of disgust, followed by thoughts as to possible amelioration. What are we to do with this disaster? On this, traditionalists and modernists can unite. Whichever form it takes, the square will exemplify that principle at its apparent worst—the classical principle of the axis, the formal composition with everything in its right place, nothing left to chance, or the modernist principle, now usually disavowed (though often deployed in other contexts), of the object in space.

p. 121

In both instances, the function is the same: to frame, to create distance, to conjure cheap games with scale and perception. No planner—whether a New Urbanist, one of those Disney-sponsored enthusiasts for the eighteenth century, or a piazza-fixated urbanist of a more high-tech stripe—would want anything to do with these giant, authoritarian creations. But is this just aesthetics, or does their hostility have any specifically political justification? Could it be the case that the uncanny uselessness of space potentially has certain subversive uses? Could it even be that these empty spaces are in fact more genuinely suited to public action and militancy than the overdetermined, 'vibrant' bustle of neoliberalism?

To answer these questions, we need to fix what sort of spaces these are, and what objects they contain. Let's take a modernist example, one easily disassociated from any direct affiliation with Sovietism: the Kulturforum in the former West Berlin. Here we have first of all a series of architecturally extremely highly wrought products: the insular, finely detailed, obsessive modernist classicism of Mies van der Rohe's Neue Nationalgalerie, whose various plinths, platforms and columns seem to encourage supplication, placing the building at an elevated remove from its surroundings; then a marooned neo-Gothic church, a mildly modernist café and, facing this, three buildings whose design was led by Hans Scharoun—the Philharmonie, Chamber Music Hall and State Library. Scharoun's attention-grabbing, demonstrative, expressionist structures sit at the corner of a vague expanse whose indeterminacy draws attention to the drama of the architecture, but does little to make the area

AN EMPTY SPACE CREATES A RICHLY...

feel like a social space. The vague, temporary feel is increased by the gravel paving. Surely it is only the prestige of the buildings, and of the exalted names of great Weimar Republic modernists like Mies and Scharoun, that has stopped planners from filling up the space with malls, housing and kiosks. As it is, the Kulturforum remains one of those last places in the contemporary city where you can still get a blast of the bracing air that once accompanied modernist city planning.

The lustrous emptiness, coldness and paranoia of this new kind of space is fervently romanticised in John Foxx's sweeping 1980 hymn to the modernist public square, 'Plaza': 'On the Plaza / We're dancing slowly, lit like photographs ... / Across the Plaza / The lounge is occupied by seminars ... / Down escalators, come to the sea view / Behind all the smoked glass no-one sees you ... / I remember your face / From some shattered windscreen'. It gets to the heart of what makes the plaza, and the Kulturforum, so interesting, and so unlike the tamed urban congestion of contemporary planning—its paradoxical official otherness, its sense of uselessness and formalism, its enjoyment of the sinister. The Kulturforum was once adjacent to the genuine wastes of the 'death strip', the lethal empty space where border guards shot at anyone trying to escape East Germany. To see what follows this approach to urban space, we need only take a short walk to the place that now fills that stretch of death strip—the new Potsdamer Platz.

An interesting urban mistake in its own right, Potsdamer Platz is an attempt to conjure up the metropolitan 'culture of congestion' of interwar Berlin, to recreate a busy commercial/traffic intersection (this was the location of Germany's first traffic lights) in the spot where by 1989 there was only windswept wasteland. The buildings, especially those by Hans Kollhoff, are finely detailed, expensive reinterpretations of Weimar-era expressionism, while the surrounding malls and cinemas try to programme bustle, refuse to let space fall empty. Potsdamer Platz strains every sinew to create movement, activity, mix of uses; that its ultimate impression is one of great coldness, seldom inspiring affection, is an enduring irony. The difference between its strained attempt at metropolitanism and the Kulturforum's quiet is fascinating; but the politics of this are more complicated than they may at first seem.

At this point, a brief prehistory of these showpiece squares is in order. If it comes from anywhere in particular, the post-war urban plaza emerges from a peculiar and often disavowed modernisation of both Prussian militaristic planning and the super-European programmatic plan of Tsarist St Petersburg, which was, it should not be forgotten, an eighteenth-century Dubai—a geograph-

AN EMPTY SPACE CREATES A RICHLY...

ically improbable project in a brutally hostile climate constructed on the orders of an absolute monarchy by the labour of serfs. Its most famous architects, Rastrelli, Rossi et al, were stars from abroad. When these Italians came to designing on this lethal, pestilent marsh in the Gulf of Finland, they took the formal devices of classicism and the baroque and pushed them to unheard of extremes. The cities of Italy or France still had an existing medieval bustle to remove before they could fit the planners' mathematical prescriptions; so too did Moscow, where Red Square's salutary enormousness gave way disappointingly to a tangle of medieval alleys. In St Petersburg no such impediment existed. Accordingly, the salient feature of the city is a boulevard of still-astonishing width and expanse, Nevsky Prospekt, leading to a Palace Square that is similarly unbelievable in its sheer size and flatness. It's as if the steppe outside this city had to be recreated at its core. Its buildings—Carlo Rossi's General Staff, for instance, with its colossal archway-entrance framing the Winter Palace—are on an outrageous scale. From here as far as the eye can see stretch buildings of an almost-uniform height, except for those considered worthy of superelevation: the golden dome of St Isaac's Cathedral, or the cruel spire of the Admiralty, the origin of a thousand Stalinist towers two centuries hence.

ACROSS THE PLAZA

This is, in theory at least, an authoritarian form of urbanism. Search 'Nevsky Prospekt' on Google Images and one thing you will most certainly find is a photograph of the 'July Days' in 1917, when the Provisional Government shot at a workers' demonstration. People are fleeing across the oversized road, with no means of self-defence, no alleys to hide in, nowhere to build their barricades. And yet, when these same workers organised the Military-Revolutionary Committee three months later, they consciously turned the city's axial planning against itself, channelling power from the boulevard to the Winter Palace. For the next few years that Palace Square, the centre of the Communist International, became the focus of unprecedented street festivals, as the oppressed of Petrograd celebrated their new power. Futurists decorated those columns and those axial office blocks with instant architectures that disappeared as soon as the festivals were over. What is curious is that later communist governments replaced this new form of ad-hoc urbanism with one that directly aped the old St Petersburg.

So why, other than sheer morbidity, would anyone want to spend their time in such places, still less make apologias for them? Current urban planning orthodoxy holds that the problem with these spaces is that they are wholly a product of authoritarianism—whether that of the Kaisers, the Tsars, or the General Secretaries. As far as it goes,

AN EMPTY SPACE CREATES A RICHLY...

this is true. They are the product of extreme centralisation, the central pivot of urban and architectural ensembles explicitly designed to instil a cowed respect for power. They are expressly designed for the mass spectacles of dictatorship, for the waving of banners, for the synchronised movements of marshalled bodies. Yet we should not forget how much those spectacles borrowed from the genuine, democratic urban spectacles of revolutionary workers' movements—the early experiments in Palace Square in Petrograd, for instance, were adopted to the letter, if not in spirit, by later 'socialist' regimes. Besides, with capitalism, we should always be very careful what we wish for. It can very easily contain, even excel at, decentralisation, disurbanism and withdrawal from the showpiece, authoritarian urban space—it has been doing so for decades. But the result is that power now resides in the exurban business park or the wholly immaterial computerised network as much as (if not more than) the central square. That's not to say that the plaza has no political power left in it. Quite the contrary.

Two remodellings of large urban squares offer some hints that the elimination of empty space has a politicised meaning. The ready-to-be-filled space of Alexanderplatz, irrespective of its top-down provenance, was the site where mass demonstrations brought down the Honecker government. It was as if the phantom public that the mass spectacles simulated had suddenly been brought to life, something no doubt rather terrifying for the DDR leadership. Over the last two decades, several plans have been visited upon Alexanderplatz, ostensibly to 'solve' the problem of its empty, allegedly unused and unusable (or more to the point, non-profit-making) space. In one of them, Potsdamer Platz architect Hans Kollhoff was asked to produce plans for skyscrapers to fill the emptiness. This plan was never officially abandoned, but instead something clumsier and more incremental happened to much the same effect, albeit without Kollhoff's formal discipline. The DDR futurism of the Platz's department store was clad in sandstone, and a series of neo-Prussian masonry-clad retail buildings have been scattered around at random: classical kitsch next to space-age kitsch. The effect is to make the place busy—to keep it shopping, to keep it consuming, rather than loitering in an unproductive and potentially politically threatening manner.

This can be seen even more abruptly and dramatically in the remodelling of Maidan Nezalezhnosti, in the Ukrainian capital, Kiev. This square was variously known as Soviet Square, Kalinin Square and Square of the October Revolution before being given its current name, using a Ukrainian term derived from the Persian for public square, Maydan. It focuses itself on a steep hill (Kiev is so replete in natural topography that the city feels almost out of place here) upon which was placed the Hotel Moskva, originally intended as a neobaroque behemoth of a skyscraper on the model of Lev Rudnev's Moscow State University or Warsaw Palace of Culture and Science. It was never completed to the original designs, so is a strange, stripped Stalin skyscraper, still with the usual gigantism and axiality but without ornament or spire. On the other side are a series of miniature towers, which also veer from full-on high-budget Stalinist opulence to something more minimal. All this remains, although the once-compulsory statue of Lenin is absent. This typical, if reduced beaux-arts Stalinist plaza (which connects to the obligatory vast boulevard, the Kreshchatyk) was the centre of a series of protests around 2000 called 'Ukraine without Kuchma', against the neoliberal-populist strongman who had been president since independence. The protesters were obstructed by the reconstruction of the square to the point where they could barely use it as a site of protest.

The result, unveiled by Kuchma in 2001, is largely a by-product of Globus, an underground shopping mall carved out of a pedestrian underpass. Its mirrorglass domes protrude onto the square in several places, where fountains and benches once were. Facing the former Hotel Moskva (now 'Ukrainia', of course) is an even bigger, axial extension of these mirrorglass structures, lined up with the hotel; billboards for the Orthodox church are placed at each end. But that's only the half of it. What really dominates the remodelled space is a series of neobaroque objets d'art—Rastrelli via Rudnev via Vegas. These fibreglass and gold structures—Corinthian columns, triumphal arches—are examples of an unmistakeable but seldom-investigated neo-Stalinist style that is extremely prevalent east of Poland: take the Cossack or Mother Ukraine off the plinth and plonk a Worker or Mother Russia in its place and you have exactly the sort of structure that would have been there fifty years ago. Officially, as with Alexanderplatz, this is to make the space more festive, more jolly, less bleak; but the aim to deter protest on this open space seemed at least implicit. Yet somehow, in winter 2004, a tent city was squeezed onto the newly congested square and Maidan Nezalezhnosti became the site of the 'Orange Revolution' that brought down Kuchma's successor, ballot-rigger and current freely elected Ukrainian president Viktor Yanukovych. And protests do continue here, although demonstrations on the square itself were briefly banned after Yanukovych's re-election. The attempt to tame the space's possibilities for political organisation failed, at least on some level; the hope of the authorities may be that sooner or later the consuming rather than protesting public will become dominant.

AN EMPTY SPACE CREATES A RICHLY...

So it is instructive indeed that the greatest revolution for several decades—the Egyptian people's overthrow of Hosni Mubarak, and the continued demonstrations that have occupied the space ever since—has been centred on Cairo's Midan at-Tahrir. This 'Liberation Square', largely constructed under Nasser, is a classic piece of Soviet-style socialist realist planning, even to the point where its most prominent government building, the aggressive ziggurat of the Mogamma, was a 'gift from the Soviet Union'. It is exactly the hugeness and emptiness of this square, and its proximity to a centre of genuine power, that has made it such a suitable place for insurrection, for being appropriated by the public in its own interest. It is also, it must be noted, the source of an enduring misapprehension that any given square can be 'turned into Tahrir Square', but a comparison with a less centralised urbanism makes clear exactly how useful the space of the square itself has been. As the revolts across the Arab world have spread, the continuing public occupation of Cairo's Soviet centrism stands in glaring contrast to, say, the difficulty of organising in an exurban, non-planned, centreless space like Bahrain. When we condemn the empty space, we should bear in mind that emptiness is often in the eye of capital and power, and that the simulation of consumerist bustle isn't much better than the still monumentalism of dictatorship.

ACROSS THE PLAZA

A similar function is performed by a phrase which is spoken all the time in this post-Soviet territory—the longing to become 'a normal country'. The meaning of this on one level is clear enough. It means wanting to be free of posturing, populist governments (Hungary's Fidesz, Law and Justice in Poland, among others), to be free of a legacy of poverty and 'backwardness', to no longer be the site of experiments, to escape from the weight of the past—to be more like the wealthy and residually social democratic nations of Western Europe, in short. But aside from the warped idea of what constitutes 'normality' (it would be news to most of the world that the affluence of France, Germany or Scandinavia are 'normal'), what is striking about this rhetoric is its closeness to that of late Sovietism itself. 'Normalisation' was the watchword of the regimes of the 1970s and 80s, after the 1968 Prague Spring was crushed by Warsaw Pact tanks. Normalisation was technocratic, officially optimistic. Normalisation didn't torture people, by and large; normalisation had no gulags, no dungeons, although it certainly had a very active secret police. Normalisation favoured the coerced recantation rather than the firing squad. Its aim was to depoliticise, to foreclose the brief possibility that socialism might have met democracy and intensified it. Normalisation promoted family values, promoted patriotism, calm, consumerism, staying in and watching telly. It is a short step from normalisation to 'there is no such thing as society, only individuals and their families'—either way, There Is No Alternative. And in most post-Soviet countries, there isn't. Throughout the 1990s and early 2000s, the communist parties (usually renamed with a combination of 'Left', 'Democratic' and 'Socialist') won resounding electoral victories across the region, only to embrace neoliberalism with all the zeal of the recent convert. With the organised left's abdication, electoral politics here veers between a protectionist, patriotic and reactionary right and a socially mildly permissive but economically harshly neoliberal right, each equally frightening in its own way. The 'Colour Revolutions' of the mid-2000s had some laudable effects—a freer press, a culture of protest—but their direct outcome was merely to change the guard at the top from pro-Russian populists to pro-US/EU neoliberals, both of them sharing a penchant for corruption and money-making. There are live movements below the surface, but it remains a hard place for an optimist.

Really Existing Urbanism charts the space of what Mark Fisher calls 'capitalist realism' as it meets the former spaces of 'socialist realism'. It registers the effects on Soviet space of two decades of a new normalisation and attempts to look a demonised landscape in the face, often finding it both more beautiful and more horrible than conventional wisdom might allow. It finds cities as they are, not as what we would want them to be. Depoliticised spaces full of harsh inequalities, strict social divides, grinding poverty and frequently hideous architecture. It also finds them full of layer upon layer of meaning, with unavoidable spatial and physical reminders that there were once alternatives, and there could still be. This part of the work, Across the Plaza, is centred on the spaces where the Soviet system was born, in a successful socialist revolution, which became the ceremonial spaces where the regimes that took the name 'socialist' displayed themselves; which were in turn the spaces where those regimes were brought down, where sometimes the regimes that followed them were brought down, and where something new could still take shape.

These spaces, with their sweeping scale, their now-inconceivable wastage of potentially very lucrative land values, are not capitalist spaces. That does not necessarily make them socialist spaces. Peter the Great also acted without the impediment of the market, capitalist relations of production or any need to take into account the needs of landowners, speculators or businesses, as Nevsky Prospekt and the Palace Square attest. That didn't make him a communist. Neither did the absence of these relations make the Soviet regimes communist in any positive sense of the term. At the same time, the dreamlike ambience of these spaces provides an

AN EMPTY SPACE CREATES A RICHLY...

attraction that is a counter to the chaotic pile-up of the capitalist streetscape. They constitute an experiment in redeveloping space according to the needs of human rather than exchange value, however 'inhuman' the results may seem—a glimpse, at times, of what we could do with cities when money is no longer a factor. The results can sometimes be merely compellingly horrible, purely cautionary; but many remain ambiguous spaces, spaces nobody is quite sure what to do with. Contestable spaces. Their exploration here will be followed by similarly itemised gazetteers on other components of really existing urbanism—the boulevard, the estate, the historical reconstruction, the social condenser, the post-industrial site, the skyline, the public transport network, the improvisation and the memorial. The eventual effect should be to build up a fragmentary, discontinuous picture of a fragmentary, discontinuous landscape.

Here, each of the squares is selected according to its particular properties, each an exemplar of a certain facet to the Sovietist square. The first, Alexanderplatz, is an absolutely archetypal post-Stalinist Soviet square—modernist in its styling but still utterly monumental—which has been subject to intensive remodelling in recent years. We move from there to the former Dzherzhinsky Square in Kharkov, Ukraine, the first major planned square in the USSR and hence a good place to try to uncover its original intentions. This is followed by Plac Defilad in Warsaw, a sort of failed square, in theory the EU's largest, in practice a vast and dilapidated car park; then we go to the non-aligned urbanism of the former Revolution Square in Ljubljana, an attempt to design small-town Gemeinschaft in Łódź, and a sort of square-in-waiting at the centre of Silesia's vast industrial conurbation. The square's darker side is represented by an enduringly unnerving square in Kiev and a space in Moscow which feels like the afterthought to enthusiastic traffic engineering. We end with Potsdamer Platz, a space which is clearly a direct attempt to repudiate the likes of Alexanderplatz, replacing them with a different form of urban focal point altogether. This survey shows the square in its multivalence, both architectural and social. All have in common vast size and 'socialist' provenance, but their very different structure and very different fate suggest that we dismiss the plaza at our peril.

Given that I came to this territory from north-western Europe—from the home of 'normality' and neoliberalism itself—this text is completely and irredeemably an outsider's perspective. I can't speak the language(s), I can't read the adverts, I only know the context from sources in translation, and I can only just buy a metro token or a drink without assistance. It would have been completely impossible to write any of this without the assistance, company,

AN EMPTY SPACE CREATES A RICHLY...

translations, perspectives and arguments of Agata Pyzik. For this she has my love and gratitude. She bears no responsibility, however, for whatever mistakes it contains or whatever sensibilities it offends.

THE STEPPE STARTS HERE

ALEXANDER-PLATZ, BERLIN

THE STEPPE STARTS HERE

If there is an archetypal Soviet-style square in Europe, it may be Alexanderplatz. Other contenders are either components of boulevards rather than squares in themselves, or they are pre-revolutionary in derivation (Red Square, most obviously). If we begin here, with a pure archetype, we can see how the others relate to it and how our final example dissents from it altogether.

p. 122

Berlin-Alexanderplatz's reputation already precedes it, thanks to novelist Alfred Döblin and filmmaker Rainer Werner Fassbinder. Its reputation is also strictly speaking inaccurate. The place that Döblin wrote of in 1928 was slated to be obliterated then, and by the time Fassbinder filmed it in 1980, it long since had been, to the point where location shots in the Alexanderplatz itself were completely impossible. Fassbinder's TV series is a succession of interiors—a seedy rented room in one of Berlin's notorious Mietskaserne ('rental barracks'), U-Bahn stations lined with glazed tiles, canvassing Nazis and communists, and peeling political posters. Neon shop signs just outside are all we ever see of 'Alex' itself, which makes it all the more striking how clear a picture there is of this absence. The name itself sounds ineffably romantic to a certain kind of English ear. And though the landscape doesn't even slightly resemble the one that Fassbinder's characters traversed, that ear creates a certain mental picture. East Berlin. The Wall. The Cold War. Postpunk. David Bowie, somewhere, wearing a long coat and sucking in his cheeks. The sound is electronic, the architecture is modernist, the season is winter.

I ought not to take the piss, because the exoticising was all mine. Alexanderplatz was my first callow encounter with the space of this book. I had visited post-communist Prague and Budapest, but cleaved completely to their pre-1914 areas, with only the occasional freakish outbreak of 1920s modernism or 1970s high-tech on the surface, or the 1970s metro systems underground, to deface the chocolate box. It was beautiful, obviously—but the only hint that something else had happened here was how specifically capitalist the space was—every available surface full of advertising, porn ubiquitous, the inescapable sense of Everything For Sale. They were also the first places I had ever been where anyone (whether bar staff, passers-by or beggars), hearing me speak English in an English accent, had assumed I was richer than them. I was on the dole or a student, but even then it was probably the truth.

I reached Alexanderplatz via the low-cost airline, that most invaluable of neoliberal innovations, taking a train there from the former East Berlin's Schönefeld Airport, whose tinted glass curtain wall grid provided a small rehearsal. Out of the window along the elevated S-Bahn tracks scrolled a still-scarred city of steelworks, power stations, the largest and greyest housing estates, punctuated by a series of lugubrious railway stations encased by yearning, arched ferrovitreous sheds, whose names were geographically unambiguous. Ostkreuz. Ostbahnhof. As I went along, the tape ran—Bowie's Berlin Trilogy, of course, but 'Heroes' rather than Low, a grimier, more manic record, its relentless disco pulses alternating with gauzy Teutono-Turkish soundscapes. It was so perfect for what I could see that I almost felt I was imagining it all. I hadn't expected this. Surely it had all been cleaned up by now, surely by now it looked normal? Then another of those dramatic iron and glass sheds for Alexanderplatz, and I got out.

It was very very cold, and the space was very very big. A TV tower was behind the station, the tallest thing I had ever seen, a faceted silver ball on a spike, impossibly futuristic. The buildings around the station were more prosaic, but nonetheless interesting for that—grimy grey grids in a style which was a little too formal to be modernism as understood in the UK. They were caked in graffiti, which added rather than detracted from the effect. Nearby was a peculiar revolving clock, a future-oriented timepiece which told you where you were in relation to Kamchatka or Vladivostok while an atomic sculpture sat on top. An extraordinarily long office block delineated the square's northern extremity, decorated with sans serif writing that I later realised was a quotation from Berlin-Alexanderplatz itself. But in between was that bloody enormous space, unlike anything I had experienced, and not merely in an architectural sense—this was December, and the gulfstream was a long way away. I gathered my scarf and overcoat around me and sucked in my cheeks, although this time not for aesthetic effect. This was exactly the place I had dreamed of, a seemingly harsh and bleak landscape whose bracing scale and emptiness felt liberating. Something could happen here. Something had happened.

Since then I've gone back to Alexanderplatz many times, now knowing what to expect. I now have some command of this place's history. Alexanderplatz was originally a circus more than a plaza, at the centre of a working-class district in Berlin's East End. Even at the time of the first Berlin-Alexanderplatz in the late 1920s, it was a hotly disputed place, a place of police beatings and assassinations. Just round the corner was the Karl-

THE STEPPE STARTS HERE

Liebknecht-Haus, the office of the Kommunistische Partei Deutschlands (KPD), the republic's third party and the largest communist party outside the USSR. Döblin's/Fassbinder's hero Franz Biberkopf, a murderer newly released from prison, was more drawn to the KPD's Nazi antagonists. The other mass political party, the governing social democrats, under their planner Martin Wagner, staged an architectural competition to completely demolish and rebuild the Alexanderplatz, receiving a plethora of dramatic modernist proposals. Wagner chose something in between, a scheme by Peter Behrens, whose formal blocks I had seen caked in graffiti on my first visit here; his scheme was only half-finished by the time the Nazis came to power, and they did not complete it, leaving it as one half of a circus. In the 1950s the German Democratic Republic chose this place—the heart of working-class Berlin, after all—as their showpiece, their public face, their grandest civic gesture, the centre of 'Berlin, Hauptstadt der DDR'. Half a mile away a neoclassical Stalinallee was constructed to lead to it, but by the time construction started on the square itself in the 1960s architectural fashion had changed sharply.

The DDR's Alexanderplatz, the one we see now, bears little relation to Wagner's and Behrens' effort, although it too was modernist and based on sweeping everything else from sight—this decidedly aided by saturation bombing in 1944–45. In front of the station and Behrens' Weimar blocks was a large cleared space, which was filled with a couple of little monuments—a fountain with abstract sculptures, the aforementioned clock. On the east and north edges, office blocks, one for the Berliner-Verlag, with a dramatic stairtower, another with that long quotation from Döblin. A third block has a flurry of sculpted reliefs, abstract and repetitious at one moment, vividly figurative at another, where stylised cosmonauts strive in three dimensions—by 2008 its top floor sported a techno club. Another still had until recently a series of red fins upon it, giving its blank façade some rhythmic movement; the whole building has been slated for replacement for some time, but there isn't much this financially embarrassed city can do with it, save for stripping those red decorations off. There are rather more impressive buildings towards the Stalinallee, the most striking of which is still the clipped steel and glass tower of the Haus des Lehrers ('House of Teachers'), decorated by a vividly coloured mosaic showing the pedagogues of the Socialist Republic. This connects to the dome and precise glass pavilion of the Congress Hall; both were designed by Hermann Henselmann, who was also responsible for the stretched-Schinkel towers of the Stalinallee. Behind the station, meanwhile, is the TV tower, a structure designed after yet another Henselmann blueprint; it meets the ground with a tangle of concrete spiders' legs. Flanking it are enormous housing blocks using the famous/notorious Plattenbau technique, an especially reductive form of system-building. The technique appears at its most comic extreme in another Plattenbau block near the Berliner-Verlag, which is literally a series of concrete boxes visibly lumped one upon another. Here you can see why Plattenbau chic is such a fetish for Berlin hipsters—it's so cute, a child's mental image of industrial construction. The empty expanse picks up again, this time flowing past the neo-Gothic Rotes Rathaus, an isolated remnant of the world before 1961, to the Marx-Engels-Forum.

Although this is (or rather was) a square all of its own, it can't help but feel like a continuation of Alexanderplatz. The very name of the place indicates that this was one of the more ambiguous post-Soviet spaces. Until very recently it featured an oft-photographed monument to the founders of communism, whose calm if slightly cranky appearance earned them the nickname 'The Pensioners'. For much of the 90s, the statues bore the graffiti'd legend 'we are blameless'. Indeed—and there are reasons other than poverty for why these statues survived so long. German unification is, ironically, probably in part the reason why German socialism survives in some form—the SPD was co-founded by Friedrich Engels, after all, though it is doubtful he would have recognised Gerhard Schroeder as a natural heir. In a country which still maintained an attenuated version of the social democratic settlement, it was harder to brand all socialist thought as an insane utopian error, a sleight of hand much more easily performed to the east, where syndicalists, Luxemburgists, Trotskyists and social democrats had long since been proscribed, imprisoned or simply massacred. The Left Party fuses ex-communists and ex-social democrats, and is part of Berlin's governing coalition. Accordingly East Germany's Marxes endure, though the Lenins are long gone. The Pensioners were recently moved from their forum—but relocated rather than demolished—to make way for a new U-Bahn station. It wasn't really them that made the forum anyway, but the series of steel stelae around them showing the vitality of international communism (as of the mid-1970s, at least)—the photographic images of Vietnamese or Latin American communists etched in indelible black onto the metal. With a couple of faces rubbed off after they fell from grace.

Alexanderplatz itself, however, is also the subject of new construction. The Kollhoff plan envisaged making the square a 'normal' part of the city once more, partly by delineating it with roads—a bizarre move on the part of a city otherwise so refreshingly oriented towards public transport and cycling—and partly by filling the new space with buildings. When these arrived, they were by lesser,

THE STEPPE STARTS HERE

journeyman architects, although the first move towards the new Alexanderplatz was actually made by a very respected architect indeed, Josef Paul Kleihues, who designed the cladding of the Kaufhof department store. This happened even before my first visit, so I had to consult archival photographs to see what it originally looked like—a box with a faced steel pattern like that on the ball of the TV tower. Given that the hostility to Alexanderplatz was often urbanist as much as architectural in inspiration—the space was simply a mistake, an abortion that needed to have people, noise, buildings, commerce, life programmed back into it—it's funny that the new Karstadt is basically the same building: an illegible box, with shops inside. This time, though, it is a neo-Prussian box, depressingly redolent of the Third Reich's middlebrow stripped classicism. The fame of Albert Speer has given the Nazis' architecture a notoriety it hardly deserved; with a couple of exceptions, it was dull stuff, with neither the icy elegance of Italian Fascism's architecture nor the demented, domineering eclecticism of Stalinist aesthetics. And why this should have been revived on this spot, of all places, is a mystery.

The two new buildings follow suit, up to a point. Both are buildings for commerce of some kind, and that's not entirely gratuitous. For East Berliners Alexanderplatz is the centre of the city—not Unter den Linden, Friedrichstrasse or the Ku'Damm, let alone the hipster oasis of Kreuzberg. It was always the place to go and do the shopping, for electrical goods, groceries, whatever. This is what gave the square the life it visibly had in its largely unreconstructed form. And this is also the source of the remarkable cheapness of the new architecture bestowed upon it. Kleihues excepted, the usual stellar standard for Berlin was not replicated here; there's the undeniable feeling of sops for the proles. The Alexa Media Mart is a case in point, a pink stone thing whose vaguely neoclassical bracing looks towards the new Prussianism as much as bristling golden cladding looks back to DDR futurism. It's a bizarre little mishmash, with what looks like a painting by Kandinsky or Moholy-Nagy on one of the façades as some kind of gesture at the modernism of Weimar. It at least has some ideas, although it is a shame they were all applied at once, which is more than can be said for the Saturn store, a blank Miesian block enlivened with panels of the building-code-approved masonry. Both buildings are rather squat, with that shamefacedness about scale and space that so often mars twenty-first-century European architecture.

On one level, it works. Alexanderplatz is full. Last time there, on a lovely spring day, ad-hoc cafes and kiosks, a miniature German market, consumed the open space. We sat there and had a very pleasant time, enjoying the incongruity of all this beer hall jollity in front of Behrens' severe façades. While a few years ago the main pedestrian presence was loitering on the fountains or lingering around the public loo, now the place was positively bustling. Of course it'd be silly to lament this. Why shouldn't people use it? At the same time, one part of the newly congested square featured an open-air exhibit on Die Wende, the change, the Fall of the Wall, acknowledging the central role that the mass demonstrations here in 1989 played in forcing the Party's eventual suicide. Looking round, though, you wonder whether the demonstrators could all fit in the space as it is today. They'd be tripping over sausage stalls and media marts. The commemoration of the revolt is perhaps what is stopping the revolt from recurring.

CONSTRUCTIVIST SQUARE

PLOSHCHAD SVOBODY, KHARKOV

CONSTRUCTIVIST SQUARE

When you leave Derzhprom metro station in Kharkov, Ukraine, you can see the Soviet square's first draft. It's the nearest thing to a truly constructivist square across the territory of the USSR, the only public space that is a remnant from its first, most open, internationalist and cosmopolitan decade. The first thing you notice is not just the scale of the plaza, but also a peculiar indeterminacy. It's in two parts, really—one of them, best seen from the furthest edge where it joins a fairly normal main road, is a relatively normal, albeit enormous plaza, a cobbled expanse that is not clearly either road or public space, between two gigantist neoclassical buildings of High Stalinist provenance. After the shock of the size, the second salient aspect is something apparently more prosaic—the Lenin statue, one of innumerable mass-produced figures placed in every single Soviet town, usually several in each; this one at least had the virtue of replacing Stalin.

p. 123

Kharkov is one of the host cities of the 2012 European Football Championship. In 2011 a promotional video showed the square without its central stone figure, as if it might have put off UEFA, Western visitors, whoever. Elsewhere they would have actually demolished the statue itself—but in Kharkov it remains. Aside from his towering, superman-style carriage—like most Lenin statues, this one implies that underneath his suit is the body of a prize fighter, rather than an itinerant, ascetic intellectual—the pose is what is so striking. His arm is outstretched towards the towers behind him, as if to say, 'Look here, this is what I have created!' Walk past Lenin and there's a green space, clearly planted so long ago that it's now very lush, with lovely overhanging trees. Here the buildings form a near-circle of rectangular concrete and glass towers, interconnected by high walkways. Here in the middle they look symmetrical, elsewhere they become an instant metropolitan skyline. This is Derzhprom (Ukrainian), or Gosprom (Russian), itself.

It would be tempting to concentrate on this building rather than the square itself—it is one of the most remarkable buildings of the twentieth century anywhere, an improbable, incredible forgotten modernist landmark, a multi-level mini-metropolis. You get a preview of it in the metro. You have to purchase a little, round and extremely cheap plastic token to enter; they're usually worn and chipped after years of use, funnelled in and out of the ticket barriers, bearing the marks of millions of fidgeting fingernails. On one side, the token displays the M symbol and

CONSTRUCTIVIST SQUARE

the legend 'Kharkiv'; on the other, the image is of a futurist building as out-of-time as the 70s-futurist metro itself.

The building is made up of several towers at angles to each other, linked by skybridges; the tallest tower has a radio mast attached to it. At the bottom of the moulded plastic relief is a framing train track and the M sign again. Even if you're not on your way to Kharkov to specifically look at the building, you might have noticed this structure earlier, as an emblem of the city on the menus of the Kiev–Kharkov express train, where it is clearer, sweeping and dramatic above the various meat cutlets and pickled vegetables. If you'd never seen a photograph of it before, you'd be amazed by the image, like a constructivist dream scheme brought to life, one of the utopian structures the early USSR could never afford (and would soon explicitly reject) that had somehow accidentally strayed into reality. Walking around the city, you'll come across its image alongside the quasi-impressionist amateur paintings on sale to tourists in street markets—it's the symbol of this large but internationally obscure city (roughly the size of Warsaw or Hamburg), its Kremlin, its Reichstag, its St Paul's. Kharkov seems to hold this uncompromising, unornamented, dramatic but seemingly un-populist square in extremely high esteem.

Gosprom—its typically Bolshevik acronym is a contraction of 'House of State Industry' —was the result of a competition proposed by Polish Soviet Commissar and former head of the Cheka (Secret Police) Felix Dzherzhinsky, to give the city a governmental complex befitting the capital of Ukraine. For this is what Kharkov was at the time—as an industrial, loyally Bolshevik city, it had gained preferment over untrustworthy, nationalist Kiev. Since Kharkov lacked the buildings to serve as a capital of any kind, this square's inception was designed to beef up this provincial town, to make it into a modern, Soviet and bureaucratic centre. Gosprom had of necessity, then, to look like the central building of a capital city, the sort of centrifugal Stadtkrone that dreamers such as Bruno Taut had speculated about, and to incarnate some sort of specifically Soviet and socialist value system, as opposed to Kiev's eclecticism and neoclassicism. The chosen site was an area of unused land—a tabula rasa—around Kharkov University. The outline plan for the square, which had Dzherzhinsky's support, was designed in 1925 by the young architect Viktor Trotsenko, and combined the axial symmetries expected of a prominent government building with something more avant-garde. Whereas Alexei Shchusev's Lenin Mausoleum of a year earlier was a compromise between an utterly ancient, dynastic image and a touch of Malevich's less earthbound suprematism, with the former clearly winning out, here

CONSTRUCTIVIST SQUARE

the order is reversed, with any hint of classicism immediately compromised by the strange forms of the prospective buildings, suprematist objects made up of interlinking tubes, lozenges and polygons. At the entrance to the circular plaza are two rectilinear towers, leading past various cubistic buildings to the central green (with statue) and the central walkway and tower complex. The complete circle of buildings was to enclose a plaza on the same preposterously huge scale as Petersburg's Palace Square or Moscow's Red Square, no doubt also specifically designed for mass events and parades. After Dzherzhinsky's death in 1926, the square was named after him.

The first phase, the building now known as Gosprom/Derzhprom, was designed by Sergei Serafimov, Samuel Kravets and Mark Felger in 1925. It is ruthlessly powerful modernism, made up of hard and stark, angular and glassy concrete forms; the very large windows and the break-up of the massing into discrete parts stops the complex from becoming as authoritarian as it might be. The building's three parts are interconnected with skyways at multiple levels, from the fourth floor to the eighth (derived, perhaps, both from fantasy and from built examples such as the skyway of the Wrigley Building in Chicago). The highest of the interlinked 'skyscrapers' reached a mere twelve storeys. The one element in this otherwise scrupulously non-hierarchical ensemble that perhaps antagonised more theoretical constructivists was the symmetry of the central entrance, with what almost resembles an unornamented concrete and glass arch, but the multi-level roofline and the round plaza's subtle curves mean the building appears to have no 'centre', and no ostensible 'meaning' — though fanciful rumour had it that from the sky, the plan was designed to resemble the stave of The Internationale's first note.

Gosprom came through World War Two intact, despite repeated attempts to blow it up. After failing to do so, the Nazis kept animals in the towers. But later phases of the plaza suffered far more from Kharkov's brutal history. The second and third parts, originally in a similar style, were damaged and reclad with heavy masonry, closing up the large windows, affixing ornament to the smooth concrete surfaces. They are still visibly non-classical in plan and roofline, though the Party House that terminates the square, once modernist, is now completely unrecognisable, recreated wholly as an imperial and Stalinist edifice. After the war, one final addition to the square was contemplated — a stepped Gothick tower, this time of genuinely American skyscraper height, akin to Moscow's 'Seven Sisters' or Warsaw's Palace of Culture and Science. It was never built, though a gigantic painting of it standing proudly as a backdrop to heroic scenes still forms

CONSTRUCTIVIST SQUARE

part of Kharkov's railway station. Perhaps as a less expensive vertical focal point, a telecommunications mast was added to Gosprom's highest tower in the 1950s, and more recently neon slogans and strip-lighting have been placed on the flat roofs (given that both were envisaged in the 1920s, it's hard to resent either).

The square itself was very clearly designed to accommodate the street festivals of the early revolutionary period, something reflected even in the plan, in the way the rectangular square protrudes into the circle and seems to invite an organised public streaming into open space. Given that there are no longer any parades, any choreographed mass festivals, to fill it, it might seem at first to have entirely lost its function, and hence feel like a folly, something that exists at a scale this economically devastated post-industrial city can no longer accommodate.

As we walked towards the square, we noticed a clutch of four middle-aged women—coiffed, coutured and shod in the dramatically spiky footwear that seems fairly obligatory for female Ukrainians—posing in front of Gosprom. Evidently, these were important people—local dignitaries, businesswomen, actresses, maybe even politicians—as there was a small group of photographers trying to make sure their pose was exactly right. This, then, is the sort of building against which the inhabitants define themselves, an emblem for them and the city itself.

ACROSS THE PLAZA

By way of comparison, the Bauhaus, a structure of comparable size and provenance, feels like a peripheral, almost suburban and basically alien presence in Dessau, an East German city which seems prouder of its handful of Wilhelmine civic edifices than for being the home of one of the most famous buildings of the twentieth century. Somehow Serafimov, Felger and Kravets created something here which inspires identification and civic pride.

The possible reasons for this become clear when you walk around Gosprom itself. The Bauhaus overhead bridge might have housed a real office, but it's at a low level and undemonstrative. Gosprom, in contrast, is exorbitant, revelling in its melodrama. As you walk under the six skyways that traverse the two roads that pass through Gosprom you might, if you were feeling especially pernickety, wonder whether there really is an entirely functional requirement for something like this; but more likely the immediate effect will be one of exhilaration. The circular plan means that the rectangular walkways fire off at unexpected angles, with the blocks curving round to meet them, never feeling obvious. It has the dizzy thrill of an imaginary Fritz Lang city that is palpable, that you can walk through and touch. Not that you'd necessarily want to, given the state of the place. The entrance to the square has been painted a gleaming white and the windows have been faithfully replaced, but after traversing

CONSTRUCTIVIST SQUARE

the first walkway, you notice the painting got abandoned halfway through, and the concrete is crumbling. At the other side the building is randomly patched up; the mildly modernist housing project that faces it is in an even more parlous, decrepit state, with ad-hoc emergency additions and tacky signs lobbed onto it. By comparison Gosprom has got off very lightly.

Any thought that the square lost its function after 1991 is suddenly dispelled when we return past Gosprom, through the encased, classicised completions of the circle. Something is assembling—fleets of taxis, crowds of people are taking the lower part of the square, while a speaker's rostrum is being erected on another side. Without the language skills to decipher it all we wander off; but on the way back at night, we stop again in the square to find it turned into another kind of instant city—a tent settlement where young people are camping in aid of a cause, much as they had in the 'Orange Revolution' on Kiev's Maidan Nezalezhnosti a few years before. One of the tents bore a helpful placard listing their demands in English, Polish and Russian as well as Ukrainian, though the English slogan, 'Fairness is our choice', didn't offer much of a clue. Later it transpired that the protest was both against tax rises on small entrepreneurs (hence the cabbies) and the disputed re-election of Kharkov's city administration; the protest placards referred to the latter as 'the Pimp of Kharkov'. Whatever was happening, it was a reminder that these plazas, supposedly open only to spectacle, contemplation or windswept recherché aesthetic enjoyment, still have a political function.

Before leaving we picked up two artefacts which seemed to confirm our thesis that here, somehow, a hard-line modernist building had managed to insinuate itself into the affections of the public. One was a painting at a stall in Rosa Luxemburg Square, a lovely green space looked over by golden Orthodox domes, depicting Gosprom on a particularly sunny day (it was on sale alongside other paintings of gleaming cathedrals and cobbled streets in the rain). It shows the aesthetic of socialist realism — the adaptation of impressionism into a fixed, monumental style — grappling with the depiction of modernism. As we buy it the painter tells us what a glorious day it was when she painted it, pointing out to us the lighting effects on the leaves, concrete and glass — the constructivist green city belatedly creating its own folk art. A few days later in the capital we found another, more mass-produced object, a Soviet-era paperweight made up of two jaggedly suprematist polygons, with an image of Gosprom and the Lenin statue encased in Perspex — modernism eliciting its own ornamental commemoration. And why not? What makes Gosprom so special is its refusal to be tasteful, 'high' architecture. Rather than being

CONSTRUCTIVIST SQUARE

anything so prosaic, it is the partial realisation of a dream, of the notion that the Soviet Union could become a socialist America, a dream of abundance, of a conception of space which entailed streets criss-crossing above the pedestrian's head, a conception of the city that meant Manhattan skylines emerging in a matter of months, and a conception of modernism that entailed a vertiginous collision between archaic longings and futurist imaginings. It is a constructivist folly, and as a folly it carries perhaps better than any other structure the vertiginous hopes that state once brought into being.

FORMER SQUARE
PLAC DEFILAD, WARSAW

FORMER SQUARE

There's a 1956 Polish newsreel called Great Gathering, showing an action in Warsaw's Plac Defilad. Enormous, unruly crowds sweep into the square, to the point where it seems the entire city has assembled in this one space. As the crowd sways and buckles, you wonder if someone might get hurt; people climb onto the lamposts to get a better view. On a speakers' tribune, swamped by the crowd, is Władysław Gomułka, new head of the Communist Party, brought to power amidst workers' protests. The commentator on the newsreel describes the site as 'the biggest parade square in Europe, which some thought could never be filled ... now the crowd is even too big for it'. It would certainly be hard to fill it again, as it's now a car park.

p. 124

The reason I can even attempt to write about Central-Eastern Europe is that I live partly in Warsaw. The Polish capital is some kind of midpoint of the area of 'transition'/Comecon/New Europe (delete according to preference), its urbanism poised precisely between Moscow (the immensely wide streets, the monumentalism, the ultracapitalism) and Berlin (the informality, the pleasant calm and slight depopulation), although I can't say that's why I'm here. My earliest memory concerning Plac Defilad, the Parade Square, is of a snow-covered expanse, with the 'Eastern Wall', a shopping centre slathered in giant ads ('Life's Good', read one of them) on one side, and the Palace of Culture and Science, a skyscraping unrescindable gift from the Soviet Union, on the other; in between was a large tent, with a street market inside. Statues of workers and peasants look out at H&M models in their knickers. It is an emblematic space.

Of all the large showpiece squares developed under 'really existing socialism', this one is surely the least likely to intimidate anyone. Plac Defilad (originally planned as Plac Stalina) was designed to frame the Palace of Culture and Science, a notoriously domineering structure that is itself the size of several city-blocks. Given that it is also the sixth largest square in the world and the largest square in the European Union, its non-presence is unexpected. Yet when walking up the boulevard Marszałkowska, or exiting the Centrum metro station, you would perhaps need to be reminded that it is a planned public space at all, rather than a random piece of post-Stalinist urban kipple, a shabby surface car park that has somehow found itself at the heart of the Polish capital (and, as the shiny new office blocks all around make clear, the

FORMER SQUARE

heart of Polish capitalism). It can be a shock to find a picture of the square clear and new, a void at the heart of the city drawing attention inexorably to the Palace of Culture and Science. Yet this effect occurs even without the construction of any permanent new buildings on it, in stark contrast to an Alexanderplatz or a Maidan Nezalezhnosti.

Plac Defilad has its history, a particularly rich one; it was here that Gomułka proclaimed the start of the Polish 'thaw', here that Wojtyła conducted mass masses, and here also that one of post-89 Warsaw's most symbolic spaces of anarchic capitalism emerged, in the form of a famously unpicturesque instant market hall that took up much of the square. Today, the main thing of note is the car park. It is partly underground, with the entrance at the square's symmetrical centre, and is generally well used, though the paving is uneven and random, partly in cracked tarmac and partly in incongruously expensive stone. From here you can approach up the steps to the Palace of Culture and Science, where you will find a square-within-a-square that is directly part of the palace itself, separating some of its (several) wings. Here too you can find the neo-Renaissance statues of heroic workers, Polish notables and symbolic figures, but you're now no longer officially in the square.

The square itself will go, sooner or later, and there have been plans to fill it for decades. One proposal by local populist politician/populist architect Czesław Bielecki entails a colossal decapitated head of Stalin as part of a Museum of Communism (which would also needlessly entail the replacement of the lovely Museum of Technology), others involve a massing of skyscrapers to finally kill off the palace's dominance over the Warsaw skyline—a dominance only reinforced by the towers that cluster on the west side of it. A surprisingly non-Bilbao, non-blingy building designed by Christian Kerez for the Museum of Modern Art has planning permission, as do more improbable, vague proposals for wonky skyscrapers, but that's about it. When the site was cleared for the museum, that meant clearing the tented street market. Riots ensued. What is there now is improvisation and accident, or rather improvisation and accident hitting militaristic, if unfinished planning.

Walking round the Plac Defilad you can find much evidence of the ceremonial functions it once had, although not for terribly long; as the building of the stylistically high modernist Eastern Wall and its environs only five years later implies, the Polish Communist leadership after 1956 were perhaps as uncomfortable with this place as anyone else. Possibly more so, as it was built for them. The largest thing in the square is the speakers' tribune, an attempt to conjure up the effect found at Red Square, where the rostrum atop the

FORMER SQUARE

Lenin Mausoleum provided a sombre, atavistic effect for the surveying of assembled tanks and missiles. The tribune is nearly, but not quite on an axis with the palace itself, so the main speaker has the palace's stone-encased steel pinnacles rising above him, and can thump his fist or gavel on the granite platform with a large, stylised Polish eagle under him, its talons tensed; hierarchy meticulously animated. It invites a thousand posed tourist photographs, but strangely it seldom seems to provoke them — probably because it's hiding in a car park. Then there are the grandiose lamp fittings, stylistically congruent with the palace in their slightly surrealist spiky-bulginess, then the cheap-and-cheerless 90s surface entrances of the metro, and then two temporary objects that say an enormous amount about the state of contemporary architecture.

Both are on the site of the Museum of Modern Art, itself not yet under construction. First, there's the barracks for the construction workers who are building the long-overdue east—west extension of the Warsaw metro beyond its current single line. A long shed, enclosed by a low, green corrugated metal fence, with a shipping container next to it, somehow escaping the vogue for container chic. When the likes of the Palace of Culture and Science and the MDM district were condemned in the second half of the 1950s as a Stalinist perversion

ACROSS THE PLAZA

of the norms of socialism—skyscraping fol-de-rol surmounting vast and unusable ceremonial space—the counter-proposal was largely centred on the prefabrication of mass housing. Prefabricated units of varying quality were built across the expanse of the Warsaw Pact states and Warsaw itself. Though concrete frames with vaguely irregular cladding are now the norm for office and housing blocks here (much as everywhere else), prefab survives, as does repetition and order, but as another improvisation, something that is not to be looked at, something that is emphatically not architecture. Move along now, nothing to see here.

Except there is here a fragment of what was supposed to replace this hyperactively authoritarian form of urbanism—unpretentious, cheap, technologically enabled housing for the workers, which was then built en masse, for good or for ill. It doesn't get built anymore. What does get built is things like the other temporary building next to it. This is also lightweight and prefabricated, but it is architecture, for sure—it constantly reminds you of that fact, so you can tell. A pavilion in aid of Poland's turn as EU President, it is a piece of attenuated deconstructivism, folded planes no doubt inspired by an attentive reading of Gilles Deleuze: wilful form-making, designed to catch the eye moving past at speed. This is what modernist architecture is today, far too often—with neither the social aim

FORMER SQUARE

of mass housing, nor the tortured melodrama of massive eclectic stone-clad edifices. Little works of self-proclaimed art, placed in the corner of chaotic spaces of accumulation and speculation.

SQUARE AS SMALL-TOWN SIMULACRUM

STARY RYNEK, ŁÓDŹ

SQUARE AS SMALL-TOWN SIMULACRUM

The supposed inverse of the overbearing Soviet square is the small-town market square, the one state-driven, colossal, domineering, the other commerce-driven, human-scale, endearing. It is curious, then, to find that the Soviet Empire at the height of its barbarity in the late 1940s was capable of recreating the small-town square with the greatest of ease, when it wanted to, when it was useful to do so. Such is the Stary Rynek in Łódź, a space which should, in current urban planning theory, be a vibrant counterpoint to the grandiose plazas.

p. 125

It is often an error to assume that the demolition or demonisation of Soviet spaces can be ascribed to a hostility towards Stalinism as such. Scratch the surface a little and you find that it is often architectural and aesthetic axes that are being ground. In Berlin, the main target of the city's post-Wende planners was the Palast der Republik, the red glass parliament/bowling-alley that marked the end of the expanse that ran from Alexanderplatz to Marx-Engels-Forum. It was a kitschy but dramatic 1970s structure which could very easily be imagined in Stockholm, pop modernism rather than authoritarian monumentalism, the product of a regime that was harsh, for sure, but no longer one of mass deportations, gulags and purges. The planning of real Stalinism, the aesthetic of the regime at its most near-genocidal, could be found instead at the former Stalinallee, whose classical axis, traditional (albeit mutant) street plan and 'active ground floors' fit with the contemporary orthodoxy. It was renovated rather than demolished. In Warsaw, the Muscovite stone monumentalism of the MDM and Muranow districts stayed, while the freeform 'Thaw modernism' of a less demented regime, such as the international award-winning Supersam supermarket, was demolished. Contemporary planning is much closer to that of 30s – 50s High Stalinism than the technocratic, modernist regimes that preceded or followed it. That isn't intended as an insult or a direct political association – nobody is implying that the Berlin Planning Department intends to liquidate the kulaks – but simply as a statement of fact.

The paradoxical traditionalism of Stalinism, its mantra of 'national in form, socialist in content', meant that it was sometimes very sensitive to infill and rebuilding in historic contexts, as the meticulous reconstructions of Leningrad or Warsaw attest. In some cases, this led to the effective simulation of old town squares that had never previously existed.

SQUARE AS SMALL-TOWN SIMULACRUM

An example of this which hasn't had the benefit of renovation or, on the face of it, significant public affection, is the Stary Rynek (Old Market Square) in the severely depressed post-industrial city of Łódź, a one-time 'Polish Manchester'. This square is reached via a municipal park decorated with the abstract sculpture of a later and more daring era, which divides it from the crumbling, metropolitan art nouveau of the rest of the city. It initially appears to be an elegant small-town remnant, a little market square demarcated by three apartment/retail buildings, all of them on a diminutive scale, as if designed for the physically smaller people of the eighteenth century. Stary Rynek is very precisely the kind of space that is now advocated by the New Urbanists.

This school, led by planners and thinkers such as Andres Duany and James Howard Kunstler, and supported by the likes the Prince of Wales and the Disney Corporation, recognises certain unavoidable truths about the contemporary city: its car-centred sprawl is ecologically destructive; its suburban non-planning discourages community and cohesiveness; its aesthetics are incoherent and obnoxious. What it advocates instead is the walkable district, with work and leisure activities easily reached without motorised transport. This requires very high densities, with people living in much closer proximity than is now customary. It also entails an attempt to replicate the low-rise cohesiveness of eighteenth-century planning. While New Urbanism opposes many aspects of the neoliberal city, its hostility to modernism and experimentation indicates an exemplary capitalist realism. It is not so surprising, then, that even though many New Urbanists will use 'Stalinist', 'Soviet' and 'socialist' as catch-all insults for big bad modernism, much of what they produce resembles socialist realism in its more timid, contextual moments.

The Łódź square is New Urbanist in every respect. It is a short walk from the city's vast cotton mills. Its low-rise flats around well-planted courtyards have restaurants, shops and bars on the ground floor, reached by colonnades, protecting from the weather. At its centre is a market square — see, even the free market had a place here, in late-1940s Stalinist Poland! Only the fact that the square is completely empty, the emptiest of all the squares in this book, spoils the intended effect of a cohesive, close-knit community. Other histories of the place are only apparent when you stop looking at the square's pretty, if minimal Biedermeier/Polish Renaissance houses and look down on the ground, where you can often see a dotted line with the legend 'Litzmannstadt Ghetto, 1940 – 44'. This denotes the former boundary of the Łódź Ghetto, where the city's Jews were rounded up before eventually being taken to the extermination camps. The

SQUARE AS SMALL-TOWN SIMULACRUM

small-town feeling is no doubt aided by the absence of anyone from outside the cohesive Gemeinschaft. Of course, although New Urbanists have an occasional tendency to say very dubious things about the innate deficiencies of tower-block-dwelling orientals, they cannot be associated with this; nor can the planners of People's Poland who built this place after 1944. But small towns are so often hostile towards outsiders.

The architecture is simple, plain and pretty. To the east and north is a pair of two-storey blocks with red hipped and tiled roofs, with folksy little openings near the top; at the bottom are the colonnades and restaurants. The more interesting part of the square, where its political provenance is revealed, is on the other side, Ulica Podrzeczna. Here are two more colonnaded low-rise blocks, also pretty, minimal and a little folksy. The folksy details bear close investigation. Much of it is simple exercises after Polish Renaissance design—free-style fluted columns, sgraffito patterns and balconies. However there are murals, too, and these depict the absent public of the post-industrial city. Each of them shows the Łódź working class at its trade: the bricklayers who built the place, the metalworkers who made the Renaissance balustrades, the miners who dug the coal that heated it. Others are more surprising, such as the lady chemist with bottles and test tubes, or the workers taking a break to admire their own handiwork—a worker and peasant in a field with factories in the background look on with contentment. The style of all this sgraffito work is distinctive for its lack of the domineering, Michaelangelo-esque muscular physicality of much socialist realism. Although it has an obligatory and now rather unnerving optimism, it feels as cute and small-scale as the architecture. There's no escaping who built it, still, but what is also inescapable is that the factories that the inhabitants could once have walked to closed some time ago; the radiantly optimistic representation of their parents' or grandparents' jobs seems like a queasy joke.

One of the murals shows the tools of the trade—two hammers and a sickle, dressed on each side with flowers. The Soviet symbol has been defaced rather than removed, half of it torn to reveal the cheap plaster underneath. It's hard to tell whether this is a specific anti-Russian or anti-communist protest or just another facet of the building's disintegration. Almost all the buildings in Łódź are in a state of advanced decay, whether modernist, classical or Gothic, and these are no exception. The open colonnade linking two of the blocks is in an especially dire state. The ground-floor shops are long since closed, and paint and plaster are flaking over every available surface; the moulded decorations on the ceiling look as if they might fall on your head. There are parked

SQUARE AS SMALL-TOWN SIMULACRUM

cars and satellite dishes, and post-Smolensk Polish flags hanging from the built-in flagposts, so the apparent depopulation only exists in the public spaces. This place, a convincing simulation of the architecture of an imaginary pre-modern community, does not appear to be any more successful at eliciting the appearance of that community than a more apparently 'inhuman' space would be; less so, if anything. Architecture can only do so much.

SQUARE OF THE INDUSTRIAL METROPOLIS

RYNEK, KATOWICE

SQUARE OF THE INDUSTRIAL METROPOLIS

Poland is a polycentric country. Unlike, say, the UK, where London is over four times the size of Birmingham, its nearest competitor, or, closer to home, Russia, where provincial centres empty and Moscow becomes ever more gigantic and dominant, it has multiple 'capitals'. Warsaw is the seat of government and finance, but it is forced to coexist with the similar-sized cities of Krakow, Poznan, Wroclaw, the Tricity of Gdansk, Sopot and Gdynia, and the conurbation of Silesia. In terms of urban area rather than official city boundaries, the largest city in Poland is in fact Katowice, the centre of the Silesian industrial conurbation. This has been acknowledged at local government level, with Katowice and its surrounding towns run as one Silesian Metropolis; there were brief attempts to rename the whole thing Silesia, as if one city. If this conurbation, itself multicentric, has a civic centre, it is the Rynek in the middle of Katowice, which is, very nearly, the dramatic, proud, instantly memorable centre this industrial behemoth deserves; though it is hard to imagine it surviving for long in its present form.

Rynek means market square, and is also the name of a more famous square in nearby Krakow, a historic, 'authentic' civic space that is everything the contemporary town planner could possibly desire. It contains a Renaissance market hall, a Gothic guildhall and basilica, pavement cafés and horses and

ACROSS THE PLAZA

carts for the tourists. The similarity in nomenclature is usually not considered to reflect well on Katowice. The Silesian metropolis is based on coal and steel, much as it ever was; it actually stretches outside Poland altogether into the Czech Republic, where the city of Ostrava provides a similarly sprawling, polycentric, industrial form of urbanism. But walk around the centre of Ostrava on a Saturday and you'll find something considerably more desolate than Katowice on a Sunday. There's a short answer to this conundrum—Ostrava closed its mines, Katowice did not, and so maintains a liveliness that is deeply unusual in a Central European industrial city. There is little celebration of this fact—efforts at 'regeneration' seem to consist in the usual creative-class courting, plus a frankly bizarre attempt to sell this dense, smoky, teeming place as a 'city of gardens'. All the same, this is one of the more optimistic-feeling of these spaces.

p. 126

The Rynek is officially just a roundabout, but it can be conceptualised more as something that gradually overtakes a typical late-nineteenth-century

SQUARE OF THE INDUSTRIAL METROPOLIS

industrial town and propels it into space. Under the railway bridge, a dense town plan suddenly opens out into something much wider. The trams pass between landscaped public plazas—the streetscape was clearly still Wilhelmine at some point (the city was part of the Prussian Empire, and has been both Kattowitz and Stalinogrod in its history). Big, spiky, wilfully grotesque redbrick commercial palaces and offices surround the roundabout on the site of the original, small-town Rynek that once stood here. Marvellously urban, they are usually neo-Gothic, neobaroque or some combination of the two, or a more sober classicism seen in the Silesian Theatre. But then larger, stranger structures start to take over. One of them is 'Zenit', a 1958 'Thaw modern' office block with department stores on the ground floor. Architecturally, it seems almost entirely unaltered since the 1970s, from the dated sign to the worn grey and yellow patterns of the main facade. The one obvious alteration is not really part of the building itself, but a series of giant adverts draped across the long, repetitious facade, blocking the light of the office workers.

This is the first proper mention in this text of something that is unavoidable in the city centres of 'really existing urbanism'—ubiquitous giant advertisements. These can almost be charted on a west—east graph, going eastwards from Germany, where they are controlled and tamed, to the Czech

ACROSS THE PLAZA

Republic or Hungary, where they grow larger and more aggressive, to Poland, where they become gigantic canvas draperies pulled across entire housing blocks and offices, to Ukraine and Russia, where the largest, most historic or important of buildings are constantly obscured by regularly updated hoardings. It feels less like some gleeful post-socialist embrace of commerce and capital, and more a consequence of total defeatedness, a shrug of the shoulders that it is normal for your flat to be obstructed at all times by an advertisement for mobile phones. These are not the pulsating neon advertisements you might find in Piccadilly Circus or Times Square or, in their greatest contemporary expression, the pulsating selling lights of contemporary China. They're static billboards, adverts you might otherwise see on a mundane hoarding or even in a magazine, printed out onto canvas on a ridiculously huge scale. Unlike the neon light, they have no attraction, no glamour, no futurism to them; they're another piece of urban waste, a ubiquitous kipple. They invariably represent Western companies and Western products, dispensed from the centre into the periphery, very often simple translations of already existing Western ads, although to be fair the products in question are more likely to be manufactured here—especially in Katowice—than in the West itself.

'Zenit', cute as it is, is no masterpiece. Its covering is not a desecration but a mundanity of one sort

SQUARE OF THE INDUSTRIAL METROPOLIS

overlaying the mundanity of another era. It is sadder to see the same process on the building opposite, the Galeria Skarbek, which is draped with exactly the same monumental T-Mobile advertisement as 'Zenit'. Architecturally, Galeria Skarbek is a dynamic Polish version of the 70s Anglo-Saxon high-tech style, designed by Jurand Jarecki, an example of 70s Poland's prescient fixation on commerce and technology, until the loans were called in. Apart from the ground floor it is windowless, so at least the giant advert disease is not actively making anyone's life more miserable. Running across the building, denoting where windows would otherwise have been, are strips of patterned metal, sharp and tactile. The steel frame is on display, and pod-like glass lifts shoot up and down the façade; these were added in a recent remodelling that also imposed a giant advertising screen and more space for adverts on the top floor. The use of bright, moving 'supergraphics' is certainly more interesting than the giant canvas ads, but there's no accounting for what they depict: the galeria is currently decorated with, aside from the T-Mobile canvas, a big Pepsi sign and video ads for basketball and a School of English. Go further along past Zenit and Skarbek, and modernism starts to replace the nineteenth-century eclecticism altogether. An apartment building with a swooping expressionist pavilion as its ground floor; two hotels, the Hotel Silesia and the Hotel

ACROSS THE PLAZA

Katowice, both seemingly untouched since they were built, 70s signs and mosaics dusty but clear; a ribbon-windowed concrete block hauled up on massive Corbusian pilotis that looks in serious need of repair, although the shops on its ground floor are all polished to a sheen. Several blocks have reliefs, mosaics or abstract sculptures built into them. Throughout this space there is constant bustle, constant public movement, the benches and spaces all very well used.

Now the already spacious landscape explodes, distances become bizarre, the scale ludicrous. This is one of the most amazing urban ensembles in Central-Eastern Europe, a blast of uncanny power, both a whirlwind of mechanised movement and a space of almost eternal stillness. A tremendous expanse, demarcated by buildings of a radically reduced, elemental character, clearly designed to be contemplated from a distance, to be seen as pure platonic objects as much as functional buildings. To the east, there is a renovated housing block, an almost absurdly wide and expansive unité d'habitation, far longer than it is tall (and it is very tall). Mercifully it has no giant draperies on it, though logos are mounted on the top floor: Centrozap, Mobil, Bisset, Agata Meble. Construction work is taking place in front of it, presumably in order to soon obscure the inhabitants' view of the central space.

SQUARE OF THE INDUSTRIAL METROPOLIS

This space forms part of the Silesian Uprisings Monument, designed by sculptor Gustaw Zemla and architect Wojciech Zablocki—one of the largest Communist-era monuments to survive in Poland, due to its impeccably patriotic theme, a celebration of the successful insurrections against German rule that took place in these disputed territories after the First World War, before their incorporation into the newly independent Polish state. Hulking, abstract and brackish in form, it couldn't be less like the run of patriotic monuments. Three massive bronze wings (one for each rising)—their contoured, outstretched membranes pointing out in different directions, like creepily organic, bulging flags— mark the furthest end of a sloping plaza, which juts out towards a roundabout, with pedestrians relegated to a series of underpasses which follow the roundabout's sweeping curves. The raised plaza on top is rounded off with granite, into a steep artificial hill, a sculptural object in its own right. It is obviously intended for state manifestations of some kind, but it is hard to imagine an improvement on this empty state. When you look past the Risings Monument towards the buildings in front, the full power of this space seizes you. This is really a Silesian Brasilia, an architecture of such spacious, concentrated purity that it is some sort of great unheralded modernist ensemble. It's possible that Niemeyer's elemental Three Powers Square was an inspiration here, although it was evidently heavily processed by the architects into something wholly Central European and industrial rather than sun-kissed and Latinate. At the end of the plaza is a clean-lined Miesian office block and Spodek, an especially sweeping, finely wrought example of the 'concrete flying saucer' genre.

The tower and the sphere. The two are in fact quite far apart, divided by some kind of square-within-a-square, but they feel like part of the same structure, surely envisaged to complement each other as well as the Risings Monument and the unité d'habitation. The tower includes the local offices of Solidarity and Virtus Finanse; it meets the ground with another abstract sculpture, a deconstructed suprematist wall. Spodek, designed by Maciej Gitowt and Maciej Krasinski and engineered by Wacław Zelewski, is an arena of improbable, Cyclopean dimensions, a remarkable piece of engineering whose ability not to fall on the heads of passers-by is notable in its own right. Opposite this cantilevered crustacean is a somewhat lumpen steel building that is hardly fit for this company. It houses restaurants and a contemporary art gallery, though its main draw is that it provides quite a vantage point for the Rynek in its totality. A fountain and benches are seemingly put there specifically for that purpose, and there's a lot of surprisingly laid-back strolling and resting, at the centre of this

SQUARE OF THE INDUSTRIAL METROPOLIS

whirlwind of movement. From here, the arterial roads fan out to the rest of the Silesian metropolis, each of them lined by concrete housing estates. On one side they are relatively modest, decorated with more canvas drapings—Levi's, repeated—and on the other, they are taller and more arresting, angular towers with star-shaped ground plans or patterned blocks with empty frames for hoardings on top. Also in this direction can be seen the source of Katowice's apparent vitality, as well as the coal dust that coats many of its buildings—the open steel framework and instantly iconic wheel and tower of a coalmine's pit head, around the same height as the high-rises, many of whose inhabitants must surely still work there.

It is, perhaps, absurd to feel optimistic about a place because it's got bloody working coalmines in it, as if that was something special. Perhaps it is only something that a Western European, familiar with the consequences of deindustrialisation in his country, could possibly feel good about, given that he is never likely to work down one. Nonetheless, a comparison with those nearby cities that have decimated or destroyed their industry tells its own story. Katowice is a living city, which in itself is very unusual in the field of really existing urbanism. And the Rynek is surely the centrifugal force at the centre of it. The city authorities may concentrate instead on gentrifying the Wilhelmine neo-Gothic shopping district nearby, with pavement cafes and a zero tolerance policy for the homeless—but this is the space unique and captivating enough to truly serve as the basis for a place that is, in real terms, one of the European Union's largest cities. It's the natural place to be built up into a metropolitan centre, a fact clearly acknowledged by new construction— a nearby multifunctional office block housing banks and a hotel. It is the potential foundation of something truly spectacular, but at the same time it could very easily find itself effaced, with an identikit Central Business District appearing in its place. It will not be easily normalised.

THE NON-ALIGNED SQUARE

TRG REPUBLIKE, LJUBLJANA

ACROSS THE PLAZA

Yugoslavia is something which people on the left tend to think about less than they should. Many like to imagine various counterfactuals about what might have happened if Imre Nagy in 1956 or Alexander Dubcek in 1968 had managed to prevail against the Russians in the loosening of Party control, the liberalisation of cultural life, and the encouragement of free speech. What they tend not consider is that it might have resembled what happened after Tito defied the Russians in 1948. The model of the Warsaw Pact reformers was often Titoism, with its artistic free expression and relatively permissive censors, its anti-Stalinist Stalinism, its still fascinatingly open-ended experiment with workers' self-management, although of course not its replacement upon its demise with a particularly bloody revanchism. The former Yugoslavia is the place, aside from Germany, where the proverbial Western leftist feels most that when he is talking about socialism his interlocutor knows what he means. Yet it was, at least in economic terms, probably the least socialist of the lot; self-management notwithstanding, the existing uneven development of Yugoslavia was accelerated under the 'market socialism' introduced in the 60s. This is partly why it now contains, to put it bluntly, both the ex-'communist' country most enmeshed in the European Union (Slovenia) and those with the least hope of eventual EU membership (Serbia,

THE NON-ALIGNED SQUARE

Kosovo). Here we will be in the former—a country that culturally feels like an extension of Austria, and economically essentially is, and its diminutive, famously beautiful capital.

p. 127

This chapter concerns a square designed and planned by a team led by the architect Edvard Ravnikar from 1960 to the early 1980s. It was built as Trg Revolucije (Revolution Square) and renamed Republic Square in 1991 on Slovenian independence. Names aside, it's a space which shows the differences between the 'socialist architecture' of Yugoslavia and that of surrounding countries; something both more internationalist and more regionally specific is present here.

You first get a sign of its rather extraordinary architecture from the 30s boulevard next to it, where the Ayn Rand moderne and Mendelsohnisms built under the preceding right-wing dictatorship are ruptured by a mammoth brutalist housing block, an asymmetric ziggurat with prickly, detailed brickwork, cantilevered balconies and what looks like vaguely medieval turrets, all with appropriately Babylonian hanging gardens spilling from them. Part of it, by being so ornamental, with its hints of Amsterdam School or a rough, proletarian art nouveau, seems to prefigure some of the less annoying elements of postmodernism—but whoever designed the lumpen 90s hat that sits on one of its wings was more literal. The stepped brick structure that faces the main road becomes something straighter, more rectilinear, as it turns towards the square, where it aggressively confronts some 30s luxury apartment blocks.

Ravnikar was a former student of Jože Plečnik, the most/only famous Slovenian architect, one of those few twentieth-century classicists who managed to create something genuinely new—a fragmented, dreamlike neoclassicism of randomly arranged stone, columns whose rustication runs out halfway up, sheathing extraordinarily atmospheric interiors. Ravnikar went off to work for Le Corbusier before returning to socialist Yugoslavia, but after the early essay in Plečnik imitation that is the Gallery of Modern Art, his work seems to have little obvious allegiance to either of his tutors. It has no Corbusian truth to materials, no classical references, however elliptical. If anything, the references sometimes seem British, with a combination

THE NON-ALIGNED SQUARE

of verdigris, brick and brutalism that evokes Basil Spence, and planning which suggests the Barbican, though the vocabulary is more original than either.

As a showpiece for the Yugoslav Socialist Federal Republic of Slovenia, it combines several different functions, all of them seemingly conflicting. There are two tall office blocks, the tallest in Slovenia, one of which used to be known as Iskra, the Spark, the name of Lenin's first newspaper — they are clad in metal, with a triangular footprint, with upper storeys in copper; there's an art gallery, a conference venue, a concert hall (Pat Metheny gurns out from the posters), a shopping mall, restaurants, various monuments and an (earlier) parliament building, most of this on multiple levels. Time has been a mixed blessing to the place, aside from the renaming. The shrubs and creepers are perfect complements to the brutalism, the purple Mediterranean-resort gating that is placed around at random less so. If there is something particularly Corbusian here, it's the use of a clear promenade architecturale, the cinematic feeling of movement between several levels, the changes of mood and material that develop alongside, from the wide open space of the plaza (converted, against the architect's wishes, to a car park, although a pleasingly empty one) to the enclosed, shadowy underground restaurants, to the subterranean mall itself.

The mall is especially lovely, on two levels,

both completely underground and in the semi-underground mezzanine carved into the square—a futuristic space that is recognisably part of the whole through the angular concrete pillars that are repeated throughout. It accommodates very well the paraphernalia of high-end twenty-first-century commerce, with only the quality of the design and materials and the subtlety of the lighting giving away its heritage in an earlier era. This is apt enough, as Ljubljana was always one of the most affluent parts of Yugoslav Federation, as it remains—a calm, quiet and, in the centre at least, clearly moneyed city. Outside of Berlin, it suffers least from the giant advert disease that has taken over most post-socialist capitals.

The other part of the square, and the element that precedes Ravnikar's design, is the parliament building, planned from the 1940s on and finished in 1960. Plečnik had his own ideas about what this parliament should look like, and his proposal entailed the demolition of the city's historic castle and its replacement with a 'Cathedral of Freedom' rising to a Babylonian point. This being a bit too mental, the end result is very different—the most sober, tasteful modernism of the era, a building clad in imperishable stone with a rigorous grid, while the turbulence of revolution is limited to the outrageous vitalist outbreak around the portal. These symbolic figures, carved by Karel Putrih and

THE NON-ALIGNED SQUARE

Zdenko Kalin, are literally bulging out of the grid, a series of naked men, women and children involved in labour of various kinds, all of them heavily stylised, and all of them displaying an unusual socialist-realist eroticism—they're less upright than the norm, the men lighter and more feminine, the women with extraordinarily wide hips and voluptuous proportions. It says the same things as any of the other socialist-realist monuments (we are building, planting and assembling, we are) while stirring the parts others do not reach. The actual entrance is boarded up, but you can spend your time lovingly examining each of these very individualised figures. The beaming, contented look of one woman holding unsubtly symbolic fruit is particularly memorable.

Two other monuments occupy Revolution Square, both sculpted by Drago Trsar. One is a monument to Edvard Kardelj, the theoretician of workers' self-management, who died in 1979. The monument appears as a parade of Giacometti bureaucrats, becoming ever more abstract and depersonalised the further they fan out from the central bespectacled figure, yet all striding vaguely towards the pedestrian plaza. The other is something more extraordinary. Yugoslavia had various memorial complexes, Spomenik, erected from the 1950s to the 1980s in an abstract, frequently architectural idiom, which have turned up lately in parodic form in all kinds of Ostalgie art (I've seen one series of them remodelled in brightly coloured Perspex), in various camp attempts to exorcise their profound emotional and physical charge. This much smaller Spomenik is a Revolution Spomenik, and fuses almost imperceptible figures into a bursting, bristling collective object. Contemplating it, running your fingers along its contours and protrusions, is an experience both moving and baffling. The square itself was recently bought in toto by a Swiss company, who collect the proceeds of the car park.

CHEKIST SQUARE

PLOSHCHAD LYBIDSKA, KIEV

ACROSS THE PLAZA

There are several dozen squares that were once named after the founder of the Soviet secret police, Felix Dzherzhinsky, most of them now renamed. Even the one in Moscow has had its statue toppled and its old (hardly less sinister) name, Lubyanka, restored. Sometimes, though, you'll find a square where the slogan 'to the courageous Chekists, fighters of the revolution' is still on display, unchanged. And there are spaces where the secret police's presence in urbanism is still very much apparent, impervious to any renaming.

p. 128

Lybidska Square, as it now is, is the location of the former Ukrainian Institute of Scientific and Technological Research and Development, designed by I. Novikov and F. Turiev in 1971. We saw it on our way elsewhere, getting off one stop early because we'd caught sight of a gigantic flying saucer cast in concrete. The 'saucer' hangs rather precipitously over the street, with the rough concrete of its underside providing shade for elderly Ukrainian women doing their shopping. Its ribbon-windows, running the circumference of the spaceship, form

CHEKIST SQUARE

the swooping pivot to an approximation of a public square, one in a clearly very grim and dilapidated state. The saucer is one of several concrete UFOs of the era, their weightlessness conflicting with their construction material. It is, however, a far larger structure than just a saucer. The street frontage of large strip windows and textured concrete is punctuated by stone relief sculptures depicting various scientific activities in a kind of reduced realism. A woman with flowing hair and a diaphanous dress holds a diode in the palm of her hand; a bald, broad-shouldered man curls himself around a set of blueprints; another abstracted maiden balances an oversized atom in her hands; a male figure bends a rod of steel into a circle; a similarly stylised man peers into a microscope. Someone has painted his eyes red, most likely fairly recently.

This is modernism of some sort, maybe, but of a radically impure variety — like the total works of Stalinism, it attempts to integrate art and architecture, and both are *speaking*, both are an *architecture parlante* aiming at direct communication and reference. It is *supposed* to look like a spaceship, it isn't an accident of its constructional technologies. Those sculptures are figurative and didactic, however far they might be from the musclebound figures of socialist realism. Their role is to animate, in a straightforward way, the purpose of the building as a scientific institute. There's nothing mysterious here, nothing inscrutable. This long block joins onto a tall tower, a skyscraper/sphere combination conceivably borrowed from the unbuilt projects of the 1920s avant-gardist Ivan Leonidov, although the lack of maintenance makes it rather more corporeal than Leonidov's pristine sketches. A glass curtain wall is well detailed but decrepit, and the name 'Ukraintei' runs up the facade. From the centre of the square, the tower and the saucer are complementary, like two old drunks propping each other up.

That's the structure as built, but there is more, in the way of unplanned and ad-hoc accretions. First, there's a huge advertisement on one side of the tower — a grinning blue whale announces, in English, the imminence of 'Ocean Plaza', a development of clearly more luxurious high towers, surmounting a shopping centre. Blue glass and irregular, contorted shapes, the signifiers of contemporary European luxury. The project's website plugs it as an entertainment complex for visitors to the European Football Championship that the city will soon be co-hosting — reassuring that you can come out of the station, through a subway, and into the mall. Below these promises, a series of corrugated iron kiosks selling this and that sit in front of the saucer, and others are unfastidiously bolted onto the 1970s building. They're here because this is a centre of Kiev, of a sort. Of course

CHEKIST SQUARE

it has a proper centre, or rather several, depending on taste — the romantic, relatively touristy landscape around Andrivsky Uzviz with its gorgeously odd Rastrelli church and (here more traditionally) picturesque cobblestoned dilapidation; the High Stalinist ensemble of the Kreschatyk; the ecclesiastical — Soviet patriotic dual hilltop ensemble of the Lavra monastery and War Memorial. Our friend Oleksiy Radynski talks about this as the centre of Kiev, however, because here all of the sprawling city's points meet. We're just round the back of the 1920s railway station, which opens out to the pre-twentieth-century inner city, and near the industrial and dormitory areas to the north, west and east — a fulcrum for public transport. And just below us is a 1980s metro station of dramatic opulence, for the appropriate sense of arrival.

If this is the nerve centre of Kiev, it says some rather disturbing things about the Ukrainian capital. Oleksiy relates various urban myths about what occurred inside the tower and saucer of the Scientific-Technological Research Institute. Rumour had it that there was a nuclear reactor here, and in 1991, in the turmoil accompanying the August coup, its failure, and the declaration of Ukrainian independence, fleets of cars and trucks escaped from the tower-and-saucer with dangerous materials of unknown significance. The other buildings on the square are of little consequence, fairly standard Soviet modernism; nearby is a flyover and speculative apartment blocks in red and white, indistinguishable from their Soviet predecessors but for the incipient hierarchy in their arrangement and the shallow curves of the balconies. The other 1970s structures on the square defer to the institute; background to its foreground. Perhaps more interesting is what goes on inside. What on the face of it look like rectilinear apartment blocks turn out to be mini-malls, with spaces divided and compartmentalised by various kinds of more-or-less informal commerce, and a much-needed public toilet whose queues and cleanliness are administered as ever by the stern woman with the loo paper. The square's transport function prevents it from having much of a public presence, as the roads encircling it can only be crossed by a series of underpasses. Some effort was made to beautify the process, with folk motifs in yellow and blue tiles marking entrances and walls, but the total lack of maintenance makes it a somewhat intimidating space to negotiate. The already surely bottom-league concrete has rotted so thoroughly that in places you look down to see that what you're walking across is the grid of steel reinforcement. That little shock is as nothing against the pure intimidation of the square's central object.

The square was originally called Dzerzhinska, and most references to the square on the internet refer to Lybidska (Dzerzhinska) either to avoid

CHEKIST SQUARE

confusion or to avoid arguments: the new name simply denotes a local river, uncontroversially resisting the usual temptation to refer to Freedom or Independence in a renaming. What you immediately feel is the absence in the place. Some Soviet ceremonial squares have, for all their menace, certain leavening features — some benches, some shelter, a fountain, *something*. Dzherzhinska Square, despite its relatively diminutive proportions, was evidently nothing so jolly. It was designed with menace primarily in mind. An empty, irregularly paved space denuded of wreath-laying and parades leads at the furthest end to a monument dedicated to the valiant Cheka. A stark stone plinth alternates between a dark and a light red, and atop that are two gigantic, interlocking severed heads — one for each wing of the state, its sword and its shield.

These heads are on a cyclopean scale, but that isn't what makes them frightening. Again, this isn't socialist realism in the strictest sense: it has none of the veracity, the Renaissance-inspired anatomical precision, that aesthetic demanded. It is representational, for sure, but it is informed by the long-vanquished avant-garde in its stylisation and reduction of the human face to a series of sharp, robotic planes. As in neoclassicism, the firmly etched eyes have no eyeballs, indicating not so much Grecian serenity as the fierce undeviating commitment of the Chekist. The sculpture glowers intensely, with the city either too poor or too distracted to dismantle it and stick it in museum or reservation. There are patches which imply that graffiti was applied and covered over, but there it stands. In its way, tucked away in this semi-derelict (but decidedly bustling, inhabited) space, this is one of the most terrifying of all Soviet memorials, an image of terror that is purer than most, because stripped of the usual quasi-humanist excuses, the fragments of the Renaissance that dressed up terror in the 1930s, a terror that had long since ended by the Brezhnev era, when this was erected. It is less the monument to a present atrocity, perhaps, than a reminder that the terror was still being kept in reserve as a possible threat, something that could always be returned to, if needed.

SQUARE BETWEEN COSMOS AND CHAOS

PLOSHCHAD GAGARINA, MOSCOW

ACROSS THE PLAZA

When is a square not a square? A place to answer this conundrum is the baffling landscape of Ploshchad Gagarina (Gagarin Square) in Moscow, a clash of plan and non-plan, futurism and revanchism, imperial dreams and fumbling accidents, one of the eeriest city squares imaginable, a place which would give any urban planner today a coronary. It is hard to express precisely the strangeness of Gagarin Square, or even to ascertain how it happened. It is, far more than the relatively sane Red Square or the positively humanist Pushkin Square, the public space which seems to the present writer to best encompass the thrilling and horrible urban illness that is contemporary Moscow—a place where you feel alternately impelled to applaud and to vomit.

p. 129

Like many of the places in this book, it was somewhere we discovered by accident, when looking for something else. That something else was the monument to Yuri Gagarin, to the south of the city centre. This aberrant mutation of the common-or-garden chap on a column genre does not sit at the centre of the public space at all, but at a

SQUARE BETWEEN COSMOS AND CHAOS

distant corner of it, so it will be left until later. The first thing you reach after exiting the metro station (nothing special, by Moscow's exalted standards) is an elevated plaza, its fittings very traditional in aesthetic, with bulbous, neo-Tsarist lamp-posts, gentle patterns in the planning and planting, and small purple 'stone' walls to provide a place to sit and demarcate the bits you aren't supposed to step on. They also wall the place off from some deeply alarming-looking roads. As a result of remodellings in 2001 the area is some kind of grandiose transport collision, with a ring road meeting underpass meeting the Leninsky Prospekt boulevard, a railway passing underneath somewhere, not to mention the metro, buried at the usual bomb-shelter depth. Three of the sides are already immensely unusual. Like the New Urbanists, again, Soviet planners were at first great enthusiasts for building workers' housing in close proximity to where the workers actually lived, although this goal was abandoned as industry and urbanisation expanded from the 50s on. Here you are in extremely close proximity to a gigantic power station. That this is shocking to a Western European visitor exemplifies how much we've forgotten that, say, Tate Modern used to generate power, or that Battersea Power Station once had a purpose beyond real-estate skulduggery. But it is surely deeply peculiar, even here, to have a public square, with the lanterns, benches, greenery and winding paths that entails, abutting these smoke-belching cauldrons.

When Jane Jacobs advocated keeping industry in inner cities near to neighbourhoods, it is doubtful that she meant this. You can see, as you sit down with your shopping, four concrete cooling towers of looming, brooding power, their concrete stained with their years of emissions; behind that are red-and-white painted chimneys. It gives the place a vividly surreal feel, as if something usually spotted from a distance on a motorway has been spliced into the picture of an (unusually coloured) nineteenth-century square. The buildings around are a similar bricolage. On one side is an apartment block that is in the space between Stalinist monumentalism and post-1953 simplicity, typically dilapidated and typically with the balconies filled in by many of the residents. Ten storeys, thirty bays, vast in any other context but humble-looking here. Facing it, in line with the cooling towers, is an extremely shabby modernist high-rise. Opposite that is the relatively new Gagarinskii Shopping Mall, unusually zippy and high-tech-looking for contemporary Moscow, perhaps in tribute to the space age which its location references. Zig-zag metal cladding meets tinted blue glass and contains Marks & Spencer. The mall adjoins another metal-clad building which if it isn't a factory now, surely once was, a blue shed resembling part of a

SQUARE BETWEEN COSMOS AND CHAOS

steelworks, presumably the reason for the nearby power station at one point.

That's three of the raised plaza's sides, but our neophyte eyes are inexorably drawn to the point where the square meets Leninsky Prospekt. What you have here is a triumphal gate to postwar Moscow, a roaring monumental archway to the Stalinist imperial capital at its least modest. Moscow sponsored the construction of various of these 'Magistrale' boulevards in its East-Central Europe 'buffer zone', but the city itself has nothing as complete in its aesthetics as Warsaw's MDM or Berlin's Stalinallee. What it has instead are torn fragments of monumental schemes, their neoclassical cohesion sullied by the accretions of the Khrushchev regime, when the concern with housing the population rated higher than intimidating visitors. This triumphal gateway is nominally Leninsky Prospekt 30 and 37, two apartment blocks ending in towers, designed by A.E. Arkin in 1946. The apartments curve around, demarcating a half-circle, another square-within-a-square, or it would be if you felt able to walk to it without being run over. The opulence and mass of the blocks suggests that they were the higher-end of Stalinist construction, although it's hard not to wonder at the placing of balconies facing some of the world's most terrifying (and polluting) traffic. At the time these roads were somewhere in between square and plaza anyway, so impossible were their multiple lanes to fill with cars—something that certainly isn't the case now. Although everything here is huge, there's none of the sense of space that comes with other Soviet squares. Instead, vastness and enormous scale coexist with chaotic congestion, as if plans had been laid upon plans without reference to each other. Not that the pedestrian should complain too much—the raised square provides a lovely, safe vantage point for the madness. You can sit here and count the heroic statues on Leninsky Prospekt 30 and 37—around sixteen, by my reckoning, though at this distance you can only pick out their flowing drapery, not their profession. The architecture of the towers is Stalinist baroque at its most distorting and perverse, columns enclosing nothing, balconies without windows. Display and hierarchy above all else. Except not entirely, because a large Land Rover sign surmounts one of them. What would Yuri have thought, one wonders, from his lofty vantage point?

The place is called Gagarin Square for a reason—it isn't all grisly Stalinian blood-and-soil imperialism. A more enlightened era of Soviet architecture is visible opposite, in the form of the Academy of Sciences designed by J. Platonov in 1980, and finished in 1988. It is partly a quite simple concrete tower, albeit with a hint of bling presaging what would happen in the 1990s and beyond—golden windows, golden curlicues. These patterns

SQUARE BETWEEN COSMOS AND CHAOS

are not resolved into some Byzantine or neoclassical motif, but are an abstract tangle, wrought screens without referent. But the star here is very much Gagarin himself. His memorial—the column and the statue that it propels—is not an 'artwork', but an industrial product, constructed specially out of titanium from a Moscow factory. It was produced by a team consisting of sculptor P. Bondareko, architects J.B. Belopolskiy and F.M. Gazhevsky, with designer A.F. Sudakov, and unveiled in 1980, when Gagarin himself was long dead; a flailing regime reminding the populace of its former triumphs.

The fluted column with the man on top is fairly literal stuff, miming Gagarin's combustive projection into the cosmos. What makes it exciting is that the whole thing is cast of the same metal, one rising sheer out of the other, the jagged titanium obelisk already a stunning futurist sculpture, with the man himself modelled in such a manner that awe is constantly intermingled with laughter. He is in his spacesuit, of course, but that spacesuit is much more angular than anything he actually wore—more fetishistic, even, with its metallic ruffs and shoulder pads. No spacesuit was ever so tight as to give such a display of musculature as this, with the cosmonaut's pectorals and six-pack in full view of the passer-by. What is more realistic is the facial expression. It would not have been altogether absurd to have chosen Gagarin for the spaceflight purely because of that beatific, angelic face, and here he looks out over this ridiculous, destructive Soviet-neoliberal ensemble as if passing on his benediction, the saint of socialist space. On the ground, a large football-shaped titanium sphere is the bollock to Gagarin's self-propelling phallus, giving the date of Gagarin's flight in Vostok, in 1961; fifty years and one month before these photographs were taken, so still fresh flowers sit at the base of the monument. Only a churl could fail to be moved, as the cars thunder past and the identikit apartment blocks of the Gagarinsky Raion march off into the distance. Earthbound.

THE SQUARE ABOLISHES ITSELF

POTSDAMER PLATZ, BERLIN

ACROSS THE PLAZA

All of these squares are places where some kind of state-sponsored masterplanning and building took place. None of them are the result of gradual accretions, few of them were troubled in any significant way by the pressure of land values and individual plots, or even property ownership itself. Spaces that are state-decreed and built as one entity are largely considered to be top-down, devoid of street life, inhuman. But what do you do when history presents you with a legitimate tabula rasa, a cleared space which really was just a waste beforehand? Can you simulate the haphazard emergence of the bourgeois city out of speculation, individual plots and the vagaries of architectural fashion? And, even if you could, would it be wise to do so? These are the central questions of Berlin's much-investigated, much-mythologised Potsdamer Platz. While there was little here in 1989 but the genuine windswept wasteland of the Wall's death strip, there was obviously a great deal here before 1961. Potsdamer Platz is a mythical modernist urtext, satisfying lovers of metropolitan congestion—this intersection was lined by stodgy Wilhelmine buildings, but inside they were pleasure palaces, and outside there were flâneurs, ladies of the night and all manner of excitements—as well as Neues Bauen modernists, as another of Martin Wagner's incomplete urban reconstructions bequeathed Erich Mendelsohn's coolly curved Columbushaus, with

THE SQUARE ABOLISHES ITSELF

other tall modernist towers like Shell-Haus and Europahaus nearby. Caught between the American sector and the Soviet sector, its surviving buildings were mostly demolished, except for the minor Wilhelmine Haus-Huth, and the basement of the Wertheim department store, which was used by the techno club Tresor for most of the 90s. When Berlin's two parts were rejoined, the city administration packaged it up and sold it to four multinational investors, to much justified protest from Berlin's vocal far left, who had other hopes for what the post-Wende city might have become.

p. 130

Potsdamer Platz is widely considered to be a failure in its attempt to an engineer a new centre for Berlin at the crossroads of its once forcibly sundered western and eastern districts. Surveys have shown that it is mainly tourists who come here, largely because of the sheer weight of history on the site. The planning tries to bring back the sense of convulsive ultra-urban congestion the place once had, but open-top buses make up the bulk of the traffic. The live forces in contemporary Berlin urbanism are all based elsewhere—the anarchists, squatters and sundry hipsters of Kreuzberg and Friedrichshain or the young professional gentrifiers of Mitte and Prenzlauer Berg largely re-use Wilhelmine or DDR space. New space, as represented by planner Hans Stimmann's blank, stone-faced infill apartment and office buildings, is disdained by both of these groups for being still, cold, bland, without the properly Berlinisch spirit of flux. Potsdamer Platz represents the Stimmann style trying to let its hair down. It is marked by a simultaneous attempt at speculative bustle and urban cohesion (almost everything is masonry-fronted, and of a roughly uniform height, with the towers allowed to creep up to a naughty twenty-five storeys), but only the latter is really apparent. Of all of the squares in this text Potsdamer Platz is probably the one that feels least like organic part of the city, least like a place for public congregation and public protest, and most like a top-down imposition—which is interesting given that it is our only purely capitalist example. Not that it ever made much money—by 2008, two of the original four corporations given a parcel of the site, Sony and Daimler, had both sold up, with the whole thing a financial as much as an urbanist failure. For all that, it's hard not to warm to it, to embrace this attempt to unite the two cities circumventing Mitte yuppies and Kreuzberg 'creatives'. There is surely a case to be made for Potsdamer Platz.

THE SQUARE ABOLISHES ITSELF

It is the least 'square'-like of Berlin squares. The area in front of the transport interchange is the only public space of note (there are several private spaces, which we will come to later), and the objects scattered here are telling indeed. The interchange itself, the Bahnhof Potsdamer Platz, is among the place's most convincing pieces of straightforward architecture, a perfectly detailed Miesian black steel and glass box with a Piranesian interior. Nearby are objects of legitimation of two regimes—the German Democratic Republic and the current unified Germany. The former is a stone marking the site where Karl Liebknecht proclaimed a socialist republic during the November Revolution of 1918; the DDR laying claim to the legacy of the revolutionary Spartacists. Near to that is bourgeois democratic Germany's own self-legitimation, several fragments of the Berlin Wall left as a permanent display of how the DDR had to imprison its population for twenty-eight years. Next to it is a permanent exhibition: one image, showing the Wall's construction as American soldiers look on helpless, has been detourned by the addition of the legend 'Mexico' beneath the US Army line and the Stars & Stripes. This is the nearest thing Potsdamer Platz has to a public forum, and it is patrolled by private security wearing uniforms that seem suspiciously like New York standard issue, as if to will into being any Times Square comparisons anyone might make. If so, it's the Zero Tolerance New York of Rudy Giuliani.

Architecturally, the best thing about Potsdamer Platz is exactly its biggest problem. It isn't postmodernist, in the sense of jolly, jokey historical reference, but it most certainly is retro. All of it, with a couple of minor and unconvincing exceptions, is a play on the architecture of the Weimar Republic, when German modernism was at its height. Hans Kollhoff's eponymous Kollhoff Tower is a clinker-clad, angular and expressionistic play on Fritz Höger's 1924 Chile-Haus in Hamburg, with a similar series of spatial distortions that make the whole structure feel like it is charging into the intersection, becoming an active element in its congestion. Höger's building was an artisan's building, with those clinker bricks detailed and ornamented with an obsessive's hand; look for something similar in the Kollhoff Tower and you'll be disappointed. What makes it powerful is the fidelity of the true believer—you really could picture this striving (almost-)skyscraper appearing in the films of Fritz Lang. Like those nineteenth-century Gothicists who got so immersed in their pastiches that they walked the gas-lit streets in monastic dress, Kollhoff has turned back the clock totally convincingly, with no nudges or winks. Just in front of his tower is a reconstruction of Berlin's first traffic light.

THE SQUARE ABOLISHES ITSELF

The other towers don't share Kollhoff's conviction. The two that make up the Beisheim Center are even cleaner, less crazed examples of Kollhoff's tamed expressionism; the Ritz-Carlton is here, should you be so inclined. Pointing into the plaza's central heart—the supposedly pulsating urban moment that we are supposed to be admiring—Renzo Piano's tower for Daimler is blandly compromised, unable to decide if it is an unbuilt Weimar glass skyscraper or a ceramic-clad Stimmann office block. It's lots of fun for those who like to admire extremely precise architectural detailing, but it's an expensive kind of precision, which no doubt alienates a city whose mayoral self-description is 'poor but sexy'. More successful, perhaps, is another Piano tower—again deeply retro—that points away from the plaza. With its assembly of machine-like intersecting parts, it resembles an attempt to build one of the 1910s dream-projects of Antonio Sant'Elia—Piano here reveals himself to be every bit as much a retro-futurist as Kollhoff. It's this feeling of walking through a pre-war science-fiction set that is the most compelling thing about Potsdamer Platz—as if they decided to create here the city centre that Martin Wagner couldn't afford to build at the time, an analogue to the way that the best German post-war music (Kraftwerk, Neu!, Can, Basic Channel) felt like a continuation of something rudely interrupted in 1933.

ACROSS THE PLAZA

As if to labour the point, you can in fact walk through a projected, 3D Metropolis in the Sony-Center. Helmut Jahn's portion for Sony is the most successful bit of Potsdamer Platz, at least in terms of encouraging visitors, who can eat bratwurst or visit a rather fine Film Museum under an all-weather high-tech tent. The bare steel skeletons, glass lifts, vaulting atria and Fosteresque transparent tower are also a reminder that there were developments in modern architecture post-1933, after all. This is quite a space at night, completely empty but permanently neon-lit in order to make it feel like the real urban centre, the visitor-thronged Piccadilly Circus that it so clearly isn't. The desolate charge of it is one of Potsdamer Platz's most memorable moments.

It's at night that Potsdamer Platz is seen at its strongest, as a modern metropolitan centre that everyone is too provincial to take to their hearts: here, when it is empty but shining, the place is a noble mistake. It's only in the daytime that its true boredom shows through. That's especially the case with Richard Rogers' segment of the Daimler complex, a straggling series of over-friendly yellow-paint and red-tile cylinders and projecting volumes that marks perhaps the exact point where the constructivist-Gothic mania of the Lloyd's Building declined into the ingratiating 'features' of regeneration architecture. Rogers explicitly opposed the retro gestures of the new Potsdamer Platz, but

THE SQUARE ABOLISHES ITSELF

on this evidence had little to offer as an alternative. Opposite is a scheme by Giorgio Grassi, a series of redbrick boxes from the Aldo Rossi school of somewhat chilling architectural reduction, which seems a great deal more powerful in its glowering refusal of fun or spectacle. Then it ends, in a mess of derelict sites and empty spaces, mocking the Platz's programmed density.

The architecture may be secondary. It is really no worse than the DDR ensemble of Alexanderplatz, though it is certainly no better. It's the product of 'Europe's largest building site', but the second and third largest building sites, in Warsaw and Moscow, can boast nothing of even remotely comparable architectural quality or civic cohesion. The fact the buildings have some overarching plan is preferable to the slap-a-load-of-icons-onto-a-square that would have resulted were, say, Danny Libeskind the overarching presence rather than Hans Kollhoff. The most remarkable thing about it is that the proverbial hollowness and desolation of the Soviet square is more present here, in this corporate land-grab, than it is anywhere else. This really isn't a place of popular assembly, really isn't a part of the 'polis', and the reasons for that range from the West's and East's refusal to take it as an allotted meeting point, a specially made neutral space, to the overbearing privatisation and private security — it's probable that the city authorities are kicking themselves for evicting Tresor from the site, as that would have given it the infusion of sexy vibrant street life it so clearly wants. The demonic Alexanderplatz still happily contains techno clubs. Potsdamer Platz remains the post-Cold War urban square that feels least ripe for appropriation; the one where it is least likely that history could restart. That is, until the leases fall in.

THE SQUARE AFTER THE SQUARE

EPILOGUE

ACROSS THE PLAZA

If there's anything to 'learn' from the post-Soviet square, it's in that passage from Alexanderplatz to Potsdamer Platz, from the seemingly ceremonial, authoritarian space that allows protest, alternative culture and ordinary working-class life to exist within it, to the seemingly dynamic, commercial and democratic space that has none of the above. At the start, we asked if the hostility to the giant plazas of 'really existing socialism' was anything more than aesthetic hostility masquerading as politics, and we've found reason to reply in the negative. But that question can also be reversed. Does it matter if we find that these wide open spaces have more street life than the counter-proposals of the 1990s—2000s? They're architecturally far more interesting than they're given credit for—but what of it?

The Katowice-based urban theorist Krzysztof Nawratek has written that to lament the demise of public space is putting the cart before the horse. For sure, urban spaces that were once genuinely public have become privatised, and are largely patrolled by private security forces. For sure, you can find people walking round these privatised spaces, mingling, drinking coffee, chatting and most of all spending money. Yet without a common conception of the public, society or collectivity, the activity you can watch and participate in on the streets is meaningless. It is possible to formally recreate

THE SQUARE AFTER THE SQUARE

the agora, in the case of the Stary Rynek, or 1920s metropolitan drama, in the case of Potsdamer Platz, but it will only be an aesthetic that is replicated. They may look like squares, feel like squares, but they're really a return to a slightly different form of 'public' square, that is, the gated squares of eighteenth-century London, free to those who can afford them and very expensive to those who can't. Malls without walls.

Protests have recently occurred on the squares investigated in this text, but what sort of protests are they? In Kharkov, cab drivers protested against tax rises and young people camped out against corruption; at Plac Defilad, the owners of market stalls rioted when they were forced out for a mooted Museum of Modern Art. Their grievances are very probably just, but there's something telling there. The protesters are small businessmen asking to be given a proper chance in a capitalism that is dominated by multinational corporations and/or local oligarchs, or they are protesting against corrupt neoliberal politicians, with the implicit promise that less corrupt neoliberals will be tolerated. It contains only hints of the population banding together to reassert themselves as a public, as the 'civil society' that observers and protagonists of Central Europe are always worrying over. Likewise, only a churlish old Stalinist could resent the reconquest of public space that accompanied the 'Orange Revolution', but that quickly produced a regime largely as corrupt and soon as hated as its predecessor.

Politics happens in the square, but in circumstances not of its own choosing. At the very least, what you can't help but notice here is that the Soviet-planned squares are still the natural places of congregation and public assembly; the only two that feel genuinely dysfunctional are those which are least stereotypically 'Soviet', in post-Wende Berlin and 1940s Łódź. In East Berlin, Kharkov, Kiev and Warsaw the space that is in dispute is the space that is largely considered unfillable, an act of planning folly, a means purely for the regime's self-edification. We will find this apparent paradox elsewhere in our excursions into Really Existing Urbanism.

OTHER TITLES IN THE SERIES

BELYAYEVO FOREVER
PRESERVING THE GENERIC
BY KUBA SNOPEK

BEFORE AND AFTER
THE PATHOLOGY OF SPATIAL CHANGE
BY EYAL AND INES WEIZMAN

LESS IS ENOUGH
ON ARCHITECTURE AND ASCETICISM
BY PIER VITTORIO AURELI

CAN JOKES BRING DOWN GOVERNMENTS?
MEMES, DESIGN AND POLITICS
BY METAHAVEN

THE DOT-COM CITY
SILICON VALLEY URBANISM
BY ALEXANDRA LANGE

SPLENDIDLY FANTASTIC
ARCHITECTURE AND POWER GAMES IN CHINA
BY JULIA LOVELL

DARK MATTER AND TROJAN HORSES
A STRATEGIC DESIGN VOCABULARY
BY DAN HILL

MAKE IT REAL
ARCHITECTURE AS ENACTMENT
BY SAM JACOB

THE ACTION IS THE FORM
VICTOR HUGO'S TED TALK
BY KELLER EASTERLING

EDGE CITY
DRIVING THE PERIPHERY OF SÃO PAULO
BY JUSTIN MCGUIRK

ACROSS THE PLAZA
THE PUBLIC VOIDS OF THE POST-SOVIET CITY
BY OWEN HATHERLEY

ISBN 978-0-9929146-2-2

Printed and bound by Printondemand-Worldwide
Published by Strelka Press

Copyright 2012 Strelka Press
Strelka Institute for Media, Architecture & Design
www.strelkapress.com

All rights reserved. No part of this publication
may be used or reproduced, distributed or
transmitted in any form or by any means
whatsoever without the prior written permission
of the publisher, except in the case of brief
quotations in critical articles and review and
certain non-commercial uses permitted by
copyright law.

First edition.

The typeface used within this book is called Lazurski, it was designed
at the Soviet type design bureau, Polygraphmash, by Vladimir Yefimov
in 1984. It is a homage to a 1960s font designed by Vadim Lazurski
that was inspired by Italian typefaces of the early 16th century.

Palace Square, St Petersburg

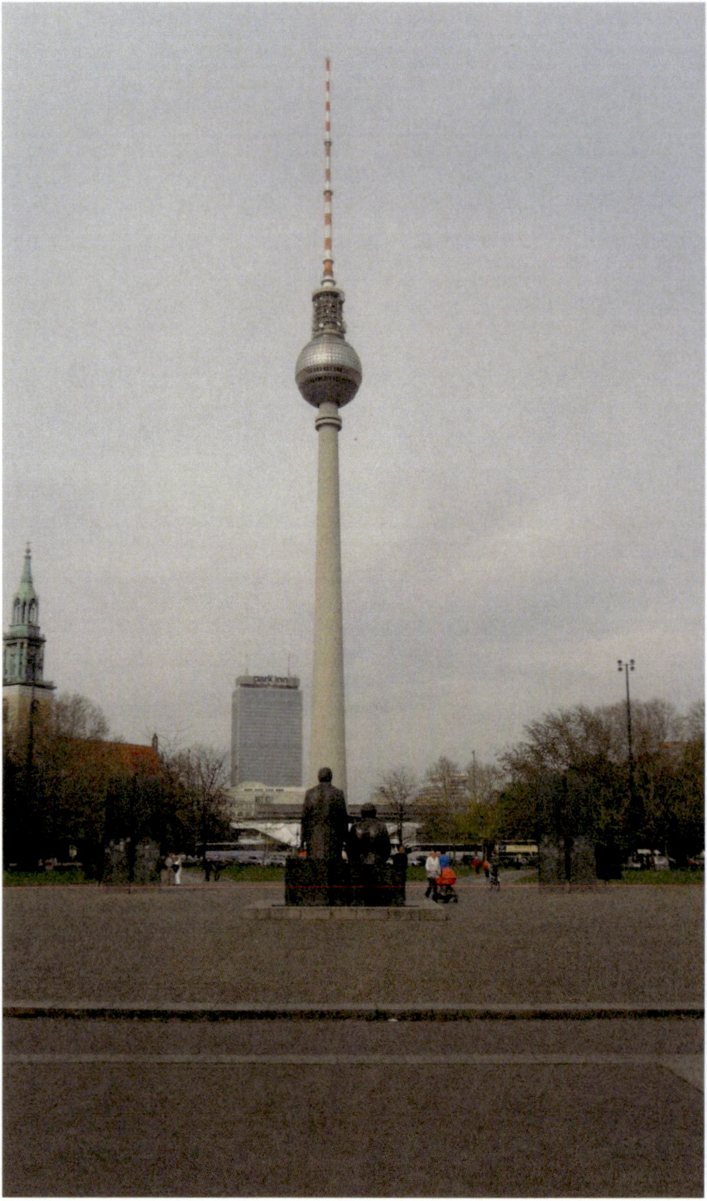
park inn

Left   Marx-Engels Forum looking towards Alexanderplatz, Berlin
Right   A demonstration assembling at Ploshcha Svobody
            (former Ploshchad Dzherzhinsky), Kharkov

Plac Defilad, Warsaw

Symbolism at Stary Rynek, Łódź

Left   Spodek and the Monument to Silesian Uprisings, Katowice
Right   The towers of Trg Republike (former Trg Revolucje), Ljubljana

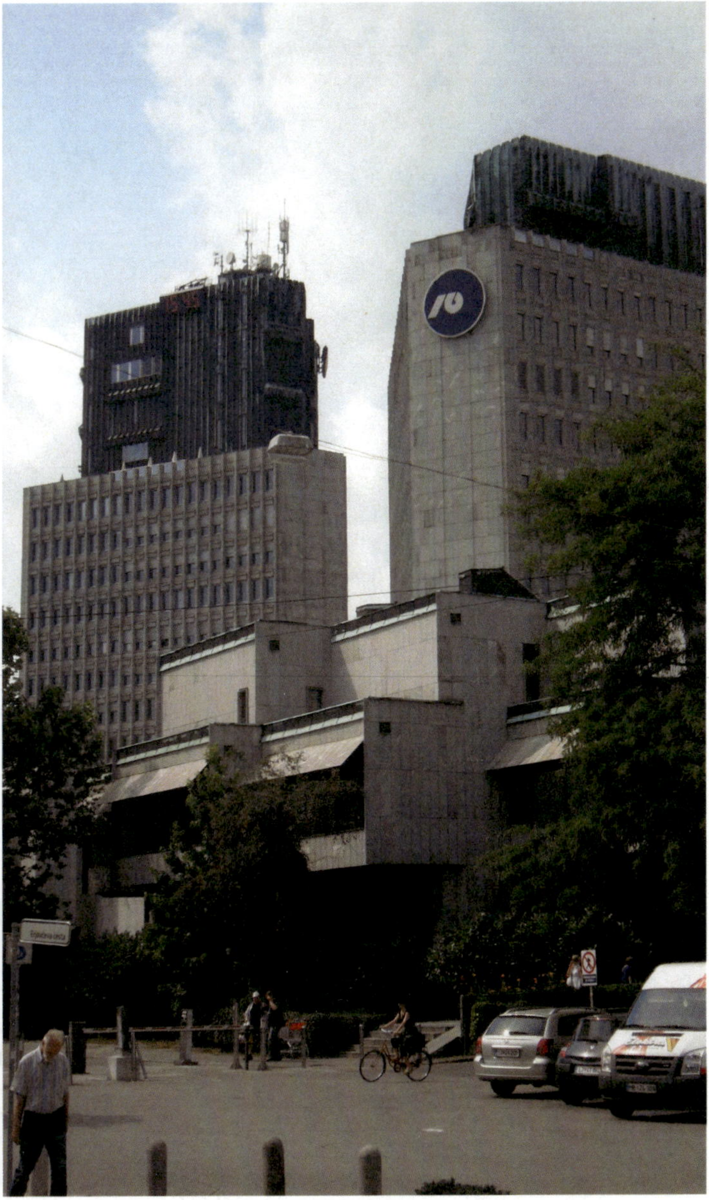

Ploshcha Lybidska/Dzerzhynskoho, Kiev

Ploshchad Gagarina, Moscow

Bleisheim Centre, Potsdamer Platz, Berlin